D1103732

EARLY SCHOOLING IN ENGLAND AND ISRAEL

|I|D|E|A| REPORTS ON SCHOOLING
JOHN I. GOODLAD, *General Editor and Director*
A CHARLES F. KETTERING FOUNDATION PROGRAM

EARLY SCHOOLING IN ENGLAND AND ISRAEL

Norma D. Feshbach
John I. Goodlad
Avima Lombard
and Associates:
Alice Burnett
Lillian K. Drag
Esther P. Edwards
David Elkind
Judith S. Golub
Else W. Hjertholm
R. Bernice McLaren
Edna Mitchell
Frances Prindle
Judith Ramirez
Lois Sauer
Joanna Williams
Robert Williams

Foreword By
Samuel G. Sava
Executive Director |I|D|E|A|

A CHARLES F. KETTERING FOUNDATION PROGRAM

McGRAW-HILL BOOK COMPANY
New York   St. Louis   San Francisco   Düsseldorf
London   Mexico   Sydney   Toronto

Library of Congress Cataloging in Publication Data

Feshbach, Norma D   1926–

    Early schooling in England and Isreal.
    (I/D/E/A reports on schooling. Early schooling series)
    Includes bibliographies.
    1. Education, Preschool—Great Britain.
2. Education, Preschool—Isreal. I. Goodlad,
John I. II. Lombard, Avima. III. Title.
IV. Series: Institute for the Development of
Educational Activities. Early schooling series.
LB1140.2.F47   372.9'42   73-14541
ISBN 07–020635–X

|I|D|E|A| is the service mark for the Institute for Development of Educational Activities, Inc., an incorporated affiliate of the Charles F. Kettering Foundation.

|I|D|E|A| was established in 1965 to encourage constructive change in elementary and secondary schools. It serves as the primary operant for the Foundation's missions and programs in education.

As an institution committed to stimulating constructive changes for the benefit of mankind, the Kettering Foundation believes strongly in the potential of education to help bring about such changes.

Robert G. Chollar
President and
Chief Executive Officer
Charles F. Kettering Foundation

CONTENTS

EARLY SCHOOLING IN ENGLAND AND ISRAEL

This volume reports on one of several studies of early schooling conducted by the Institute for Development of Educational Activities, Inc. (|I|D|E|A|), an affiliate of the Charles F. Kettering Foundation.

Dr. John I. Goodlad, director of |I|D|E|A|'s research efforts, places the need for this study in context when he refers to "the recent educational discovery of the young child." To those who know something of the history of early childhood education, the adjective "recent" may seem puzzling, but the key term is *educational discovery*.

Until about fifteen years ago, efforts at preschool education were motivated mainly by humanitarian concern for lower-class children left unsupervised for long periods, or by a belief among the upper class that, as Dr. Goodlad phrases it, early education was "not harmful and perhaps useful" for their children. Thus, preschool education was on the one hand a form of welfare and on the other a loosely defined privilege to be ranked with going to the seashore in summer and associating with the "right" families. In neither case did schooling have serious educational significance.

That concept of early schooling has changed. In our time, the work of developmental specialists such as Bruno Bettelheim, Martin Deutsch, J. McVicker Hunt, Benjamin Bloom, Jerome Bruner, and Jean Piaget has won broad assent for the proposition that the early years—those between birth and six—are crucial to the child's development. We have seen a new national interest in preschool education, as evidenced by the federal government's initiation of Headstart, by the opening of many new preschools (some of them profit-making ventures), and by increasing enrollment in private and public school programs below the kindergarten level.

Despite these encouraging signs that we are beginning to take the early years seriously, the mixed results from preschool efforts and the findings from this |I|D|E|A| study indicate that we have far to go before we match our new educational *interest* with a commensurate educational *skill*. We have come to recognize the importance of the early years in human development—but we do not yet know how to design educational programs appropriate for those years.

This lack of knowledge—in addition to the importance of capitalizing on developmental research and translating it into practice—places the study of early schooling in an institutional perspective. In considering possible preschool program directions for |I|D|E|A|, we thought it only sensible to find out what *is* being done—not only in the United States, but in a country with a long history of preschool practice (England) as well as a countr with a short history but an urgent national concern (Israel). We inquired into Asian preschool practices because relatively little is known about them and we thought that some interesting variations on western viewpoints and practices might be identified.

Finally, a thorough study of early schooling practices aimed at improving education in elementary schools was considered important to |I|D|E|A|'s Change Program for Individually Guided Education (IGE). This program tries to recognize and accommodate such differences among children as age, emotional maturity, intellectual aptitude, learning style, and all the other factors that distinguish students even in their earliest years. Clearly, the quantity and quality of a child's preschool experience (or lack of it) also required consideration; this study has helped us make judgments that have been incorporated into our elementary school program.

These are reasons for supporting this three-year inquiry—but they are not the reasons for its formal publication. We feel that the study is important on its own merits, beyond its utility to |I|D|E|A|, and that its facts, conclusions, and speculations will reward any educator interested in those crucial years of human development.

Samuel G. Sava
Executive Director
|I|D|E|A|

CHAPTER 1

EARLY SCHOOLING: AN OVERVIEW OF RECENT DEVELOPMENTS

JOHN I. GOODLAD*

Until a very few years ago, task forces and conferences on educational problems and needs, national or international in scope, paid little or no attention to children under the age of elementary school entrance. This is still the case, usually, in those many countries where establishing universal elementary schooling and maintaining secondary schooling for even a small percentage of the age groups are formidable achievements. Nevertheless, in those countries with universal elementary and near-universal secondary schooling already attained, education of the young preschool child now vies with higher education and surpasses education for the elderly in public and government interest, research, development, and experimentation. Educationally speaking, the young have been discovered.

EARLY ROOTS: ELITISM AND NOBLESSE OBLIGE

Throughout modern history—certainly since the advent of the industrial revolution—there has been some educational interest in young children. This has tended to take two forms. Some middle-class and well-to-do citizens have viewed a few hours of nursery school or kindergarten each day as not harmful and perhaps even useful for their children. Such schools assured safe, supervised play with peers and an opportunity for the mothers to gain free time for their own purposes.

* This writing was accomplished while the author was a Fellow at the Center for Advanced Study in the Behavioral Sciences, Stanford, California.

There has been evident a certain elitism, then, in early childhood schooling. At the other extreme, however, there has been visible in industrialized countries a humanitarian spark of concern for the children of laborers and factory workers, often deprived of their parents for long hours, which has been expressed through medical, nutritional, and educational intervention. There has been, then, a compensatory characteristic in early childhood schooling.

The elitist form of early schooling has found favor in both developing and developed countries. When the goal has been only to assure supervised play, socialization with other children, or relief from child care for parent, nurse, or "nanny," formal educational instruction for the young has been taken lightly. Only some philosophers or, later, social psychologists and students of child development viewed "play" as having deeper educational relevance and relationship to later development. The concern on all sides was, rather, that surroundings and facilities be healthful, that personnel be warm and friendly, and that the "right" children be enrolled to assure the desired social environment.

However, when places in the higher schools were limited or when upward mobility depended heavily on success in school, another element was added to play and games in nursery school and kindergarten. Early childhood schooling took on some of the characteristics of primary schooling, with recitations, "reading readiness" activities, and more controlled, formal, school and classroom atmosphere. "Mrs. Atwater's Pre-School for Little Ladies and Gentlemen" became just that —a pre-school, preparing for the next school—with elaborate graduation exercises marking the fact that Susan or Andrew was now prepared for school. When such preschools were not by definition of or for the elite, they at least suggested association with or attainment of an elite status for one's offspring.

Some disagreement, worldwide, can be found as to whether healthful facilities and surroundings, warm and friendly adults, and the opportunity to play and socialize with other children are or are not adequate ingredients for early childhood schooling. Until one strays beyond the confines of the favored socioeconomic classes in a society, the need for more may not be widely apparent. Confronted with slums, poverty, illiteracy, and the legacy these beget, however, one must deal, first, with the realization that these conditions of early schooling are not easily attained and, second, with the nagging query as to whether they are enough. It is not easy to provide a garden for children (kindergarten) in a Harlem slum, let alone the needed hundreds of them. It is not easy to find warm and friendly adults who love children to staff a nursery school in the ghetto, let alone thousands of them. In addition, playing exclusively with one's peers, all of whom speak a language alien to the favored one of the land—or a corrupted version thereof—does not hasten departure from the slum. Something more, indeed, appears to be needed.

Interestingly, the search for something more that so characterizes the present ferment in early childhood education owes a good part of its heritage to what has been up to now an apparently inevitable back-wash of social and industrial progress—namely, urban poverty and slums. Interest in and concern for impoverished and disadvantaged children have spawned theories, stimulated research, led to the financing of innovative and experimental educational programs, and directly or indirectly benefited the education of all children. The work and consequences of Montessori constitute a case in point. Her interest in slum children afflicted with physical and mental problems carried her beyond the conventional wisdom of her time into the development of educational programs and materials which served to guide the young through a series of sequenced learnings. Each activity, each piece of material, had its specific purpose and was designed to be used according to a plan. The present flowering of popular and scholarly interest in early schooling is nourished to considerable degree by contemporary concern with the very learning problems that motivated Montessori.

Until recently, there has been, then, a kind of bimodal distribution of both interest and enrollment in early childhood schooling, so far as industrialized countries are concerned: on one side, the middle- and upper-class interest in getting a head start in school or simply in providing wholesome, play-centered activity for their children; on the other, a kind of philanthropic or noblesse oblige concern for children caught most seriously in the backwash of industrialization. Such concern has figured very little in the development of early schooling in nonindustrialized countries, largely because poverty is so widespread that nothing short of massive programs of social engineering, for which resources are not available, would suffice. Providing schooling for a handful of the most disadvantaged would constitute an unwarranted frill.

The bimodality of interest in schooling for the young may be seen, also, in accompanying research and inquiry. Studies conducted in countries with elitist facilities have tended to focus more on child development than on aspects of schooling per se, even when undertaken by professors of education. Studies of language styles, sex differences, growth patterns, and the like are familiar to future teachers taking classes in educational psychology, for example. They appear to have been motivated more by academic interests and intellectual curiosity than by pressing social urgency. Such interests are more readily supported in a relatively affluent, industrialized society.

Interestingly, researchers in this context only rarely raised basic questions about the conduct of the preschool program itself or sought to appraise its efforts. This kind of inquiry is a recent phenomenon. Rather, investigators seem to have accepted the assumptions underlying the program in which the studied children were enrolled, if they thought about them at all. The intent, apparently, was to secure cases to observe or with whom to conduct small experiments which would interfere minimally with the ongoing program.

Unfortunately, this appears to have been the case, also, with research conducted in university-based "laboratory" nursery schools. A review of research conducted in schools of this type in the United States would reveal a long list of psychological studies into child development and a shorter list of sociological ones, but a paucity of educational studies or projects on school programs. Even solid descriptive and analytical work is in short supply, to say nothing of the measurement of experimental alternatives. The extrapolations required to leap from the conventional kinds of studies to the formulation of programs in early schooling is so great as to be exceedingly dangerous, especially if one seeks to go beyond the elaboration of general concepts pertaining to individual differences and the like. This is a most unfortunate legacy from a long-standing pattern of early schooling that helps to explain (and even to justify) the demise of most laboratory schools.

As suggested earlier, it is difficult to determine whether failure to challenge the implicit assumptions and ongoing activities of the elitist-oriented nursery school was by way of commission or omission. Joseph Schwab has pointed out both the creative thrust required and the professional danger involved in questioning the long-held principles guiding inquiry in a field. He has observed that most researchers engage in short-term investigation, safely within the confines of accepted principles. It takes a Darwin or an Einstein to engage in the fluid inquiry productive of new concepts and principles which, again, after further legitimation, become the research domain of a new generation of scholars.[1] But there seems not to have been a swirl of intellectual activity of either the short-term or long-term fluid variety surrounding the conduct of nursery schools for the middle and upper classes. To repeat, such intellectual activity as has been conducted has focused on children and child development and rarely on educational practice.

By contrast, the limited interest in retarded and disadvantaged children, an interest virtually paralleling the development of industrialization, has been accompanied by both inquiry and some innovation with respect to *programs* of early schooling. Until recently, the children of the slums only rarely attracted academicians for at least 2 reasons. First, they were not as readily accessible as children already "captive," close to where the professor lived (or where, in fact, he sent his own children). Second, such deviant children offered little for the standardization of test instruments, behavioral norms, and so on. Schooling for the disadvantaged attracted humanitarians and social reformers interested in doing something about a social problem. Those who stayed with it came up with plans, decisions, and programs, the best-known of them contributing decision-oriented, not conclusion-oriented, inquiry to our legacy of early schooling.[2] One may disagree with Montessori's view of the retarded child's potentialities, and even with her pedagogical precepts, while at the same time employing in a kindergarten materials that are direct descendants of those she created.

When an aspect of human affairs is not the subject of intense intellectual attention and excitement, the sharp impingement of new or newly discovered social conditions can effect an abrupt shift. This is essentially what has occurred in bringing about the recent educational discovery of the young child.

What has been written on previous pages regarding early childhood schooling is generally applicable, with relatively minor modifications, to most highly industrialized countries of the world up to very recent times. It is applicable even today to most industrialized countries and, with respect to the discussion of early schooling for the elite class, most developing countries. What has changed the scene so rapidly and profoundly in some countries is the emergence of strikingly new and demanding conditions.

RECENT DEVELOPMENTS IN THE UNITED STATES

In the United States, the 1960s constituted a decade of transition from the bimodal distribution of interest in early schooling described earlier to a virtually nationwide awakening to the educational potentialities of all young children. Even in the late 1950s, provision of public kindergartens was a privilege of the wealthier school districts, except in those few states providing support for a K-12 system, and the bulk of nursery school attendance represented the white and affluent. Intellectual interest in the schooling part was low. Then, the nuclear era and fear of being eclipsed in the race for outer space precipitated an upsurge of interest in schooling generally and the beginnings of what was to become an unprecedented flow of funds, including funds for research and development, in the succeeding decade. This research and development took cognizance, at least to some extent, of the early childhood years.

However, it was in the urban backwash of the technological revolution that both neglect and need became suddenly apparent. The data had been around for a long time, mostly in sociological treatises that were beginning to see the light of day in testimony before the courts. There were not only the problems of poverty, slums, and urban decay, so increasingly the story of the world's major cities, but also the problems of minority group subjugation and racial prejudices, so long kept half-hidden in a closet but now so glaringly revealed to the world as the United States' cancer. Conant has said, "This republic was born with a cogenital defect—Negro slavery."[3] The coincidence of urban slums and the residence of minority groups in them, juxtaposed against the coincidence of affluent suburbs and the residence of whites in them, posed what Conant aptly termed "social dynamite."[4] The accompanying issues remain to be worked out within the context of individual and group equality and inequality.

The educational discovery of the young child in the United States during the 1960s represents a fascinating interplay between profound social events and scholarly inquiry which deserves more extensive analysis than can be attempted here. The cold-war clash of two great powers spawned almost frenetic educational activity (and this is as true for the USSR as it is for the USA). This activity was encouraged by a national commitment to education, including allocation of funds for research and development. The latter, in turn, fed back into federal planning both speculation and hard data concerning untapped learning potentialities in the young child at the very time that meaningful, compensatory intervention in the total welfare of the disadvantaged was desperately needed. The Economic Opportunity Act of 1964 created Headstart, and several titles of the Elementary and Secondary Education Act of 1965 made provision for early childhood education, including the creation of an undernourished National Laboratory in Early Childhood Education.

Minority-group confrontation tactics also played a significant role in the awakening of interest in education. Motorists who had driven the Los Angeles network of freeways for years finally discovered Watts; citizens who sent their children to private schools in Manhattan suddenly awoke to the sickness of New York. Relentlessly, court case after court case was spelling out what had to be done to rectify long-standing inequities. As some educators have said about recent educational reforms, "The courts are where it's at."

The work of educational scholars also fueled the activity. Reacting against the "unfolding" view of child development, Bettelheim declared, in the provocative title of one of his books, "Love Is Not Enough."[5] Or, to cite Bruner, "We begin with the hypothesis that any subject can be taught effectively in some intellectually honest form to any child at any stage of development."[6] Or Bloom, "We could expect the variations in the environment to have relatively little effect on the I.Q. after age 8, but we would expect such variation to have marked effect on the I.Q. before that age, with the greatest effect likely to take place between the ages of about 1 to 5."[7] These statements effectively challenge the long-standing concepts of "letting the child unfold" which still dominated the field into the late 1950s. Current research activity is stimulated by the hypothesis that development can be modified effectively at an early age and both research and development by the challenge of how best to do so.

Whatever the components and dynamics of this interplay, however, there is no denying that concern for children below the age of 6 has entered the mainstream of social action and educational inquiry in the United States—and within the short time span of approximately fifteen years. No president or presidential candidate can afford to omit early childhood education in his plans for the country. No public school official or school board member can afford to take lightly the suggestion that schooling in his community be extended downward to the age of 5 or 4, even at the expense of other segments of the program. A first-rate group of scholars is now actively involved in research and development pertaining to the young child and his education, with an accompanying high level of intellectual ferment, and a solid body of literature is beginning to emerge.[8]

Educational discovery of the young child in the 1960s presents us with an intriguing but staggering set of problems and issues for the 1970s. Whether to intervene, in the "schooling" sense, with the child's natural developmental processes remains an issue, despite the new rhetoric. In fact, there are now two sets of rhetoric with various shades of viewpoint within each: that of the interventionists and that of the romantic, de-schooling, or free-school groups. The former group represents a range of positions from rigorous arrangement of the environment to assure practice and reinforcement of desired behaviors (with accompanying extinction of undesired behaviors) to emphasis on taking advantage of the child's unfolding in arranging rather nondirective educational activities stressing, particularly, cognitive and language development.[9] In this group, certain exponents of operant conditioning who sometimes recommend activities that are initially very distasteful or even physically painful to the children arouse antagonism among their colleagues and, as can be well imagined, provoke vigorous condemnation by those in the "romantic" camp.

The latter group includes the "de-schoolers" who deplore the prospect of very young children being caught up in what they regard to be an inhumane institution protecting and perpetuating many of the social injustices with which society is now plagued.[10] The large majority of the romantics, however, espouse the long-standing permissive view of letting children unfold in a pleasant, supporting, encouraging preschool environment. Some in this group appear to be completely ignorant of the long history back of what they espouse; they are wide-eyed with the thrill of a new discovery. Others have not looked about lately and are quite unaware that powerful, alternative ideas have entered the children's garden. Of course, we are addressing ourselves to a continuum of positions regarding schooling for the young child; the difference in practice is infinitesimal between the interventionist who believes in organizing educational activities around ongoing play and social life and the self-styled "open school" exponent who believes that children should be left alone to explore an environment that has been arranged for them. But the rhetoric of each is different.

A second set of troublesome issues pertains to where, how, and when to intervene. The search will be endless; an enormous amount of research will be required. With respect to the where, a substantial body of inquiry is directed at language and cognitive development. The language problems of minority group children are receiving direct attack. Here we have still another instance of the inquiry pertaining to disadvantaged children having a very practical, education-directed orientation. The problem to be attacked is clearly there—it is vital to the welfare of both children and society and it calls for interventionist strategies. It is not surprising, then, that much attention is focused on modeling the language patterns to be learned, producing effective materials, and evaluating the processes and effects of intervention.

Back of this decision-oriented activity is an accelerated interest in studying fundamental language processes, and this work, like the studies in cognition, goes beyond the solution of immediate problems, is less of a trial-and-error variety, and has its operational base primarily in the laboratory. However, immediately practical activities such as the designing of educational toys, language tapes, and various pedagogical procedures interface from time to time with this conclusion-oriented activity, sometimes very directly.

With respect to language learning, a troublesome problem of "when" arises out of the fact that Mexican-American children, for example, more often than not encounter Spanish as the first language of the home. Is it better to encourage more effective speaking of Spanish in the young child, followed by primary schooling conducted primarily in Spanish, before introducing speaking, reading, and writing in English? Until recently (and largely still), kindergarten and first-grade activity invariably employed middle-class American English, regardless of the specific children's language base, seriously aggravating problems of school learning for these children. Research findings will not lead immediately to solutions, since intensely emotion-producing issues of cultural pride and heritage are involved.

One of the most troublesome issues in early childhood education pertains to the lasting effects of intervention through nursery school and kindergarten. To date, studies in Sweden, Japan, Israel, England, the USSR, and the USA, for example, suggest that the effects of early schooling have washed out by approximately age 8 or 9 (grade 3); children who have had such schooling cannot be differentiated academically from those who have not. Nevertheless, this kind of inquiry is still at a very primitive stage. First, it often is difficult to know the nature of the children's nursery school or kindergarten programs. If they emphasized the natural unfolding of the child, not much in the way of specific school learnings should be expected. If the program included elements of primary school work, to be repeated later, it becomes difficult to assign cause of failure to early or to later schooling.

Second, absence of lasting benefits from early schooling does not necessarily mean either that there were none or that none are possible. Extant tests used in the schools measure only a relatively narrow range of behaviors and accomplishments. Also, perhaps stressing concept formation, motor coordination, and verbal language fluency in the early years makes a significant impact on the individual's ultimate scholastic attainment—in sharp contrast to learning numbers and the alphabet, for example. Although available evidence increasingly points to this conclusion, we have been singularly limited in devising comprehensive programs capitalizing on such an hypothesis.

This becomes apparent in the examination of the exceedingly popular children's television program, "Sesame Street." The fact that so much emphasis has been placed on reciting the numbers and the alphabet is less an indictment of the producers than it is of an impoverishment in creativity among program developers in early schooling who, however committed to basic concepts and skills they may be, seem not to be able to escape the routine accouterments of "school." Perhaps the de-schoolers have a point!

The problems of intervening for lasting benefit come sharply into focus in so-called compensatory education for the disadvantaged. Again, it is a case of sharp impingement of new or newly seen contingencies on long-standing problems of previously low visibility. Well-planned efforts at early intervention for children with limited home and community stimulation appear to have some rather immediate benefits. (Of course, those from rich environments profit even more from equal periods of educational intervention, as is to be expected.) Nevertheless, as the Israeli experience with early schooling for large numbers of immigrant children demonstrates, the withdrawal of compensatory intervention when the child enters school leaves him in a still-disadvantaged position in regard to academic learning.

This observation is leading a growing number of specialists to conclude that an effective intervention strategy must begin at a very early period; must encompass a full range of mental, physical, social, and emotional considerations; and must embrace home and parents. "Homestart" rather than "Headstart" is gaining favor as the political rubric for child-care programs.

We have said that the preceding fifteen years constitute a time of discovering the young child educationally; but how penetrating has this discovery been and how many children below first grade are now affected by it? Answering the second question first, estimates of 5- to 6-year-olds currently in nursery schools and kindergartens in the United States run up to 70 percent of the age group. The top estimate for this group in the mid-50s was about 40 percent. The current top estimates for 4- to 5-year-olds are from 35 to 40 percent. The figure was half that in 1964 and perhaps half the 1964 figure in 1955, at the very outside. These relatively large numbers of children are enrolled in regular public school systems, independent schools, college laboratory schools, Headstart centers, parent cooperatives, church-controlled schools, and so on, scattered across the country but heavily concentrated in metropolitan areas.

By "educational discovery of the young," however, we mean much more than getting them into school-type programs of one kind or another, significant though this may be. We mean capitalizing on the relatively new hypothesis that the early years not only offer challenging possibilities for accelerating or redirecting critical human traits but also may be of crucial significance in the never-ending effort to assure optimal development for every individual. The notion that exposing children to some kind of early schooling somewhere is enough, or at least a reassuring start, may be dangerously naïve.

In another volume of this series on early schooling, we report on our visits to approximately 200 nursery schools, chosen to include a sampling of all the major types currently in existence, in 9 major metropolitan centers of the United States. The findings are sobering, and the reader is urged to examine them for himself.[11] We shall not include them here. What struck us most forcefully is that the traditional and, until recently, largely unchallenged assumptions of play, games, and a spattering of academic, school-like activities still predominate. Knowledge of and excitement about the new hypotheses could not be said to be characteristic of these nursery schools. Their keepers too often brought to mind the World War II Japanese soldier who had been hiding out on Guam until early 1972 and upon discovery was startled to learn that President Roosevelt was dead.

It is quite unrealistic, of course, to expect that most nursery schools already would be implementing research findings in cognitive and language development or replicating some of the exemplar programs affiliated with ongoing projects. Change simply does not occur this quickly. But it does seem reasonable to assume that large numbers of nursery school directors, at least, would have caught some of the pervasive excitement from leaders in the field and would be proceeding on a trial-and-error basis with one or more of the several assumptions, guidelines, and procedures. A good many were versed in the rhetoric—which is a kind of occupational imperative if not the chronic disease of educators—but this proved to be only a jargon having little descriptive relationship to the familiar, long-standing nursery school practices so commonly repetitive and so clearly displayed.

This brings us to what are clearly the major problems in early schooling for this and probably subsequent decades, if we can assume somewhat optimistically that the present ferment in research and innovation will continue to be encouraged and supported, politically and financially. The first is that of attracting and educating a sufficient number of able, interested young people who will make careers of early education. A prime obstacle is an acute shortage still of leaders to direct the education of these teachers—persons of breadth and imagination who are able to free themselves from narrow schools of thought or research and extrapolate from present knowledge in developing viable programs.

The second issue, central to our entire educational enterprise, is that of mounting and maintaining self-renewing change mechanisms. Bronfenbrenner concludes his comparison of child rearing and educating in the USSR and the USA with an insightful chapter on what seems to be required. His is essentially a systemic approach, addressing itself to the problems, roles, and essential activities of classroom, school, family, neighborhood, and the larger community.

> ... Our analysis points to a paradoxical situation. Even though the lack of parental involvement is at the heart of our present malaise, parents by themselves can do little to bring about the needed change. For ... it is not primarily the family, but other institutions in our society that determine how and with whom children spend their time, and it is these institutions that have created and perpetrated the age-segregated, and therefore often amoral or antisocial, world in which our children live and grow. Central among the institutions which, by their structure and limited concern, have encouraged these socially disruptive developments have been our schools.[12]

We share with Bronfenbrenner the view that both school and family must be regarded as part of a social system that reinforces desired teacher behaviors, gives teachers a stake in the development of children under their care, provides easy access to new ideas and the opportunity to learn the behaviors implied by these ideas, and so on. For some years, we have developed and tested such a sociopsychological change strategy and are now coming to see its possibilities for addressing the formidable problem of inertia and anachronistic practices in nursery schools of the types now looming large in the futures of the unborn.[13]

The transcending paradox to be kept ever in mind regarding early childhood schooling (and primary schooling, other data show[14]) is that there is a very wide gulf between the emerging theories and ideas of our time, including those actually being demonstrated in experimental centers, and the bulk of ongoing practice in early schooling. It is as though there were two clearly identifiable strata, separated by a belt of sand through which communication is possible but by no means assured, let alone systematic. This is not a condition to provoke the gnashing of teeth and beating of breasts; in most matters, it hath been ever thus. The gulf between funded knowledge and conventional wisdom is formidable, and many of the alternative positions regarding education of the young have not yet reached the status of funded knowledge. But the situation is a constant reminder that, although inquiry into early childhood schooling may have joined the intellectual mainstream, nevertheless much of practice is still a quiet lake on the other side of the mountains. Neither eloquent nor impassioned pleas "for the sake of the little children" will do much for them, fond as we tend to be of such exhortation.

Nevertheless, systematic, planned processes of change such as proposed by Bronfenbrenner can make a difference. A shotgun approach, discharging shot across a wide range of strategic but scattered components, although politically attractive, will not make much difference. Needed is an integrated effort involving federal and state governmental action, dealing with both contingent circumstances and the substance of education; a general refurbishing of our present ragged efforts in research and development; extensive provision for teacher education, with insistence on direct laboratory as well as academic experiences; and social networks for change, involving close collaboration between local educational agencies and institutions and the home, consortia of cooperating early childhood educational centers, pedagogical service stations for updating personnel, and an array of communication mechanisms. We have addressed ourselves elsewhere to such strategies for educational change.[15]

A NOTE ON COMPARATIVE STUDIES

The problems of one's own country frequently are revealed more sharply when viewed against similar problems of another. Employing such a process is particularly useful in seeking to gain a long-term perspective. Simultaneously, of course, one secures knowledge of other places which is of interest and value in its own right.

It was with both purposes in mind—to gain perspective on rapid developments in early schooling in the United States and simply to find out what was going on elsewhere—that |I|D|E|A| launched descriptive studies of formal educational programs below the level of normal admission to public school in selected countries. The roots of early schooling in England and the United States intertwine at many points. The rhetoric in both countries draws heavily from familiar names such as Froebel (and Rousseau's *Emile* has been a favorite of the romantics in both countries). The work of the McMillan sisters in England during and after World War I with the depressed and deprived certainly made an impact on parallel concerns in the United States. It seemed appropriate, therefore, to take a look at nursery schooling today in England, particularly since the primary level of schooling there, the Infant School, was beginning to get such a play in the United States.

Israel was a "natural" for two closely related reasons. First, a volume of immigration which is virtually unprecedented, proportionately, in any country brought with it unusual problems of educating children from diverse backgrounds who were seen to be seriously disadvantaged in relation to the educational goals of the State and the arduous demands of the present and future. Second, the ambitious plans to provide schooling for incoming 4-year-olds led to some ingenious experimental activities spanning research, theory, and practice. As we shall see, however, the relationship between educating these immigrant children in Israel and educating minority group children in the large urban cities of the United States is not nearly so close as is sometimes assumed. The research and experimental activity, frequently aborted because of a shortage in personnel and funds, may be of more general interest and application, however.

We turned to Asia because so little has been published in English regarding the practices there and because Japan very well may have the highest level of preschool enrollments of any nation in the world.

These are not comparative studies in the sense of seeking to make explicit how selected aspects of organization, program, or pedagogy differ or are similar from country to country. Further, it was not our purpose to reveal relationships between commitments, beliefs, and values, and the educational systems of each country, nor to reveal differences or similarities from country to country. Our hope was, rather, that we might gain ideas and insights which would be helpful in seeking to improve early schooling in the United States. The resulting descriptive material is a kind of by-product, presented for whatever use it may be to students and practitioners in early childhood schooling.

We found at the outset, somewhat to our surprise, that comprehensive guides to detailed observation and description of practices in early schooling are hard to come by. At any rate, we found nothing that suited our purposes. Consequently, we prepared our own, a copy of which appears in Appendix A. It was used, in various stages of modification, in conducting observations in all countries. We hope it will be of use to both students and researchers in the field.

THE CASES OF ENGLAND AND ISRAEL

The initial decision to juxtapose the reports on England and Israel in a single volume was motivated by expediency: taken together, they conveniently constituted a small book. In retrospect, such a decision will be justified on more substantive grounds. The people of both countries have had a long and arduous struggle for freedom and dignity in which education has played a valued role. Both, compared with all the peoples of the world, have had a disproportionate representation of their people in commerce, international financial activity, literature, the arts, and affairs of the intellect in general. Both have maintained an intense interest in politics, often making of it an art as well as a subject of intense debate. Both have been noted for singular tenacity with respect to a cause, often respecting principle over personal survival. Both have experimented with innovative forms of government, often drawing productively from experience with and knowledge of alternative forms of government worldwide. When one thinks of England and Israel, one thinks in each case of the intellect and the part it plays and has played in the development of these two nations, one quite old by Western standards and the other very young as a state but populated with people of a long, troubled, and binding past.

The educational context in itself provides some interesting observations. In the cases of both countries, although education is highly centralized in that the respective ministries can and do establish basic guidelines with respect to the organization and conduct of schooling nationwide, local involvement and decision making are both respected and assumed. In Israel, we see this particularly in the kibbutzim, the religiously-oriented schools, and the commonly separate kindergartens "close to the people." We see it in England in the delegation of so much authority to the headmistress. The rhetoric supports this decentralization even when the actual effects of insidious government controls are clear. On questioning the obvious external control in the once rigidly applied eleven-plus examinations, the visitor to English schools was likely to hear in reply, "Yes, but the headmaster is free to run his school as he sees fit." The Jews in Eastern Europe, before emigrating to Israel, were accustomed to making all decisions, including educational ones, in the *shtetl* (small, closely knit communities), whatever the centralized authority of the ruling group.[16] Today, in England, the trend is toward further relaxation in government regulations that restrict local initiative and toward greater encouragement of parent involvement in schools. In Israel, one does not associate long with educators before hearing grumblings over "a ministry already growing bureaucratized" during the short years of its history and expressions of faith in the power of local schools to improve themselves in the face of burgeoning problems.

Because there are no separate states with substantial educational powers, as in the United States and the Federal Republic of Germany, the ministries in both England and Israel are able to effect a somewhat more direct relationship with the schools (and, perhaps, between official policy and general conduct of the schools). For example, both have centrally employed personnel who directly visit the schools, either as generalists (Her Majesty's Inspectors in England) or often as subject-matter specialists as in Israel. These structures tell us something, also, about how widespread or drastic change is sought. In Israel, a rather widely known instrument for change is the Curriculum Center of the Ministry of Education and Culture, which draws upon scholars at Hebrew University, Tel Aviv University, and other institutions of higher learning in preparing curriculum materials which become standard for the schools. Preparing teachers to use them is, of course, quite another problem which currently is left largely to other agencies.

In England, significant changes such as modifying age of school entry or the length of schooling frequently begin with special study committees whose reports are acted upon by Parliament. On becoming law, new requirements are administered by the Ministry, with Her Majesty's Inspectors playing a key role in enforcement. When a problem or need is sensed, a Royal Commission often is appointed and headed by a distinguished citizen whose name will be closely associated with the final report, giving it a special legitimacy.

One such instance, associated rather closely with our subject matter, is the so-called Plowden Report prepared by a commission headed by Lady Plowden. Unlike many commission reports of its genre, it proposed and succeeded in legitimizing to high degree a set of practices to accompany an organizational unit known as the Infant School. The report was a synthesis of beliefs regarding the education of children between the ages of 5 and 7 drawn in part from England's own heritage in early education, in part from other countries (particularly from some of the more progressive aspects of primary schooling in the United States), and from a careful analysis of exemplary ongoing practices in England and much extant theory, research, and innovation described in the educational literature.

Perhaps the time for the ideas recommended had come; there is little doubt, however, that the built-in structure for change and the process of legitimizing new ideas paid off. In a remarkably short time (the report was published in 1967), many primary school staffs were diligently at work seeking to create exemplar models of what had been recommended, and hundreds and then thousands of visitors from other lands were coming to look (and by their too great numbers to impede the effort). It is difficult to tell how successful the effort has been. Elaborate evaluation is not a built-in characteristic of English primary education. Certain critical English educators say that what visitors see and often describe with such enthusiasm represents only the best 2 to 5 percent of all ongoing practice.

It is somewhat ironic that early schooling in England was not characterized by an aura of excitement during the time the data were being collected for this report. This writer, visiting Infant Schools in England just a few months before Professor Feshbach's first period of observation, was struck by the obvious disparity between this segment of schooling and nursery schools sometimes attached. "Attached" is perhaps not the proper word—"appended" might be better. Even though the former have been widely touted in the United States for their apparent freedom or openness, there was a sense of order and direction, a tone set by the headmistress and a program emanating from the teacher. In fact, after a few visits, one was able to predict this order, the materials being used, what the teacher would do under certain circumstances, and the like—an impression that is strangely missing in many of the reports brought back to these shores by visitors to British Infant Schools. By contrast, children in the nursery schools appeared to be drifting along, with only a very limited range of activities to attract or challenge them. They played a good deal but often in a repetitive way that merely killed time: throwing a ball back and forth between two children, taking turns rolling in a barrel, over and over. Teachers and headmistresses with whom this writer talked seemed not overly concerned; this kind of activity is quite appropriate, apparently, for children under the age of 5. The young appeared not to have been discovered educationally.

Perhaps this is due, in part, to the fact that the roots of early schooling in England are deeper and stronger on the social welfare side than on the elite side. Middle-class mothers have favored keeping their young children close to them in family-nurtured activities. The Pre-School Playgroups, described at some length by Feshbach, represent a shift in view that dates back to World War I, but their very character emphasizes the middle-class view of early schooling as being closely related to the home. They are essentially cooperatives, stressing the kind of open, informal play and creative activities that conscientious parents would like to see going on around them every day among their own and the neighbors' children. But many present-day demands, space limitations, and the like make this impossible for the home environment. Parents express satisfaction with the Playgroups, in contrast to the reservations expressed by parents with children in private nursery schools. Pre-School Playgroups may mark the beginning of a renaissance in a country that once did much to stimulate interest in early schooling in the United States and elsewhere.

It is clear that immigration and assimilation are to be powerfully motivating forces for Israel's preschool activity, perhaps indefinitely. There is an urgency. The idea that the Jews must possess their own territory and become a nation, almost bizarre in 1880, became a swelling passion, stimulating the emigration from Eastern Europe of up to 30,000 Jews who came to Palestine between 1882 and 1903—and the waves continued, again and again, flowing from all over the world. Hebrew was seen as the great, tradition-steeped, unifying language to be taught in all the schools, and the State was scarcely created in 1948 before the Compulsory Education Law saw to it that there would be an early beginning, providing at once a year of kindergarten (over arguments that there should be two). Today, of course, the drive is to include that second year, by offering kindergarten places to 4- and even 3-year-olds wherever possible and by making special arrangements to provide early schooling for the newly arrived and ever-arriving children.

As stated earlier, attempts to compare the education of minority group children in the major cities of the United States with the education of Israeli immigrant children must be forwarded with caution. Admittedly, there are similarities. The parents are economically disadvantaged and are unable to provide the stimulation needed to sustain the advantages of compensatory education, once this intervention has been withdrawn. As in the United States, many of these parents speak the official language of the nation and school poorly or not at all. True, many of the most recent immigrants tend to be differentiated by darker skin. But there the similarities quickly drop off.

A comparison with a United States of an earlier time would be more accurate, a time when English, German, Swedish, Polish, Irish, and—yes—Jewish immigrants were coming to this country, wave upon wave, seeking to find a place, to adopt a new country and have it adopt them, and to be assimilated. But even here the comparison soon stops. Those arriving now in Israel have come to join their brethren and are linked by religion and the historic language of that religion, sharing in common a persecution that runs deep in history but also is very much in the mind of modern man. Staggering though the problems are and will be, these are assets and motivations that cannot be denied. Blacks in the United States have been persecuted in a country they did not choose; they sought no promised land across the seas. Certainly, there are ethnic differences and subdivisions of identity among the Israelis, but whether they ever will loom large enough to resemble the problems both experienced and presented by Mexican-Americans, for example, in the United States remains to be seen.

When one moves below these national and cultural differences, however, to consider theories, research, programs, and practices of educating young children, a dialogue between educators in Israel and the United States (and all other countries discovering the educational potentialities of the young) holds much promise. The urgency of the problems has forced some Israeli educators to give serious thought to how best to educate the young child, even while overwhelmed by the task of mounting and sustaining new school provisions. The desire to do a great deal quickly, coupled with the use of foreign consultants who have pointed to the developmental significance of the first few years of life (the Israelis have made extensive use of outside experts), has been used as support for a considerable academic orientation in early schooling. Love of children runs deep in the Jewish culture; there is equal familiarity among Israeli educators of approaches emphasizing play and rather permissively guided unfolding of the child. Also, sitting somewhat apart—but less and less in some quarters—from the frenetic activity of bustling Tel Aviv, for example, are the kibbutzim, where one may see Bettelheim's "Children of the Dream"[17] or, as Israelis are apt to describe them, "the children of the cream."

Up to the age of 7, the nongraded approach, multiage groups of children, cottage-based living together, integrated materials, and a rich supply of manipulable and other materials of all kinds remind one of elements, smoothly synthesized with elements that are unique to the kibbutz, of English nursery schools and of some of the best primary units in nongraded schools of the United States. Then, a more formal, graded program takes over, still characterized, however, by certain principles established from the beginning.

From the kindergarten near the hastily erected housing development in Tel Aviv to the comparatively long-established and stable kibbutz, the student of early schooling finds himself stimulated by a panoply of possibilities in early schooling and the many problems, issues, and alternatives stemming from them. Interestingly, some of the research and experimentation described by Lombard in Chapter 3 mirrors the possibilities arising when one considers seriously what it is best to do in educating the young. In Israel, whether one is looking at practice or examining ongoing research, the orientation reflects social urgency.

A similar urgency is absent in England, but the makings of intensified activity in early schooling are there. Only a small proportion (about 10 percent) of 4-year-old children are in preschool. The country has its share of urban children, in particular, who could profit, presumably, from a preschool year, and the number of working mothers —or mothers being newly "liberated"—looking favorably toward preschool facilities is increasing. The quality of nursery schools is showing up badly against that of the Infant Schools for children between the ages of 5 and 7, a fact which could stimulate intellectual activity regarding what best should be done for 4-year-olds. The Plowden Report had some interesting things to say about nursery schooling, but the time for these ideas was not ripe. It can be anticipated that an early report on education before the age of 5 by one of Her Majesty's Royal Commissions could find the time to have ripened considerably in the years since the Plowden Report was presented.

POSTSCRIPT

It is clear from the following reports that the problems and issues of early schooling summarized earlier with respect to the United States are by no means unique to this country. England and Israel, too, have a shortage of trained personnel, top-level leadership to prepare them, and a paucity of research and development taking one from theory to practice of schooling. Research in Israel appears to be more sharply focused on educational alternatives, whereas much in England treats of developmental factors in children. In examining practices in both countries, one is quickly confronted with the familiar issues of when, where, and how to intervene or whether to intervene at all. In both countries, improving and extending the collaboration of home and school appear to be very much on the cutting edge of approved practice.

In regard to one recent development, at least, what is happening in the education of young children in the United States appears to have no parallel in England and Israel. This is in the commercial franchising of chains of nursery schools for little ones, a phenomenon that appeared to be burgeoning in the United States as the decade of the sixties came to a close, but which appears to be slowing down somewhat in the seventies. One thread unraveling from our several reports on activity in early schooling suggests that investors in such enterprises would be well advised to look twice before promoting a boom that may fizzle.

Birth rates in the United States have slowed markedly and are not likely to increase soon, if at all. An easing of pressure in numbers to be educated is conducive to increased interest in bettering the quality of the education to be provided. Labor unions increasingly are including child-care provision for workers in their bargaining packages and management is encouraged by the effects of company involvement in pilot child-care ventures. The reports on England and Israel suggest that, for these countries at least, programs conducted close to and with parents have greatest appeal. There are increasing signs that such is likely to be the case also in the United States. Early schooling for 4-year-olds will be a public and local community matter. Increasingly, too, in rhetoric and fact, the mode for still earlier educational provisions will bring parents and educators into closely cooperative and collaborative enterprises conducted close to the home, not merely physically but psychologically and sociologically as well.

Early schooling is an idea whose time has come, but many problems and issues remain to be resolved before the provision of satisfactory educational programs even begins to match recent enthusiasm for the possibilities. The most troublesome of these everywhere is, of course, how and when to intervene constructively in children's early development, now that the significance of the preschool years is so clearly evident and widely recognized. Simply adding a lower rung to the school ladder is not sufficient. In fact, extending downward what is now done in the first years of school may be harmful. Rather, programs must be extrapolated from our growing insights into the needs and learning characteristics of young children, tested with many children, and then adapted continuously to the highly individualistic developmental patterns of each child.

England appears to be on the verge of a new era in early schooling. There is considerable dissatisfaction with current practices and a growing resolve among selected leaders to take a constructively critical look at what is required to move beyond them. Israel will be confronted with the educational needs of immigrant children into an indefinite future. The question there seems not to be whether children as young as 4 or even 3 can profit from state-supported educational interventions but, rather, how best to get results in a relatively short period of time. In all likelihood, it will become increasingly productive for the educational community in the United States to know about early schooling in both England and Israel and for a dialogue to be maintained.

NOTES

1 Joseph J. Schwab, "Problems, Topics, and Issues," in Stanley Elam (ed.), *Education and the Structure of Knowledge*, Rand McNally, Chicago, 1964, pp. 4–42.

2 Lee J. Cronbach and Patrick Suppes (eds.), *Research for Tomorrow's Schools*, Macmillan, New York, 1969.

3 James B. Conant, *Slums and Suburbs*, Signet Books, New York, 1961, p. 16.

4 Ibid., p. 10.

5 Bruno Bettelheim, *Love Is Not Enough*, The Free Press, Glencoe, Ill., 1952.

6 Jerome S. Bruner, *The Process of Education*, Harvard University Press, Cambridge, Mass. 1960, p. 33.

7 Benjamin S. Bloom, *Stability and Change in Human Characteristics*, Wiley, New York, 1964, p. 68.

8 See the extensive bibliography prepared by Lillian K. Drag and included in another volume of the |I|D|E|A| Reports on Schooling, Early Schooling Series: John I. Goodlad, M. Frances Klein, Jerrold M. Novotney, and Associates, *Early Schooling in the United States*, McGraw-Hill, New York, 1973.

9 For a summary of several major intellectual positions, see Goodlad, Klein, Novotney, and Associates, ibid., Chapter 2. Also particularly

useful are Ellis D. Evans, *Contemporary Influences in Early Childhood Education*, Holt, Rinehart and Winston, New York, 1971; Joe L. Frost (ed.), *Early Childhood Education Rediscovered: Readings,* Holt, Rinehart and Winston, New York, 1968; Robert D. Hess and Roberta Meyer Bear (eds.), *Early Education*, Aldine Publishing, Chicago, 1968; and Chapter 2 in Evelyn Weber, *Early Education: Perspectives on Change*, Charles A. Jones Publishing, Worthington, Ohio, 1970.

10 For an analysis of pros and cons, see Robert J. Havighurst and Daniel U. Levine (eds.), *Farewell to Schools?* Series on Contemporary Educational Issues, National Society for the Study of Education, Charles A. Jones Publishing, Worthington, Ohio, 1971.

11 Goodlad, Klein, Novotney, and Associates, op. cit.

12 Urie Bronfenbrenner, *Two Worlds of Childhood: U.S. and U.S.S.R.*, Russell Sage Foundation, New York, 1970, pp. 152–153. © Russell Sage Foundation. Reprinted with permission.

13 A series of papers and books reporting |I|D|E|A|'s 5-year study of the change process in schools is now in prepartion as part of the |I|D|E|A| Reports on Schooling: Series on Educational Change, Mc-Graw-Hill, New York, in press.

14 John I. Goodlad, M. Frances Klein, and Associates, *Behind the Classroom Door*, rev. ed., Charles A. Jones Publishing, Worthington, Ohio, 1973.

15 |I|D|E|A| Series on Educational Change, op. cit.

16 See Amos Elon, *The Israelis: Founders and Sons*, Holt, Rinehart and Winston, New York, 1971.

17 Bruno Bettelheim, *Children of the Dream*, Macmillan, London, 1969.

CHAPTER 2

EARLY SCHOOLING IN ENGLAND

Norma D. Feshbach

ACKNOWLEDGMENTS

As stated in Chapter 1, this report on preschool education in England is part of a larger survey of comparative educational practices and research in early childhood schooling conducted under the auspices of |I|D|E|A|, an affiliate of the Charles F. Kettering Foundation. The author is grateful to |I|D|E|A| for the invitation to conduct the study and for the support and encouragement provided throughout. The resources provided by |I|D|E|A| and the stimulation and support provided by Professor Goodlad and the |I|D|E|A| staff are gratefully acknowledged. This support made possible an unusual opportunity to observe directly and at close range a significant part of an educational system in an important and exciting country.

The author and |I|D|E|A| are indebted also to the many people and organizations in England who graciously gave of their time, energy, and interest toward facilitating this study. Their diverse contributions are reflected in the body of this report. Although it is not feasible to cite the names of everyone who helped in so many ways, we would like to thank particularly a few individuals whose help and concern were essential to the implementation of this study. Dr. Mary Waddington, Senior Lecturer at the Institute of Education, University of London, was of critical help in getting the study underway. She provided an initial perspective on the status and history of preschool education in Great Britain and made many useful suggestions as to people to interview and institutions to visit. Miss Elma McDougall, Her Majesty's Chief In-

25

spector for infant and nursery education, gave generously of her time and counsel and was responsible along with other members of the Department of Education for the thoughtful scheduling and cordial reception at the various institutions and communities that were visited. Of equal importance was the feedback Miss Mc-Dougall provided concerning the impressions received and inferences made by the author at various points during the course of this inquiry. Her devotion and contribution to preschool education left an indelible impression.

Finally the author wishes to thank her husband, Dr. Seymour Feshbach, Professor of Psychology and Director of the Fernald School, University of California, Los Angeles, for his assistance regarding the observations made of schools during the second visit to England and for his critical reading of the research section of the manuscript.

AN OVERVIEW

Early childhood schooling in England has a long and respected tradition. The nursery schools opened by the McMillan sisters shortly after the turn of the century served as a model and stimulus for nursery education in many western countries, including the United States.[1] However, the current state of preschool education in England does not reflect the leadership and innovative role this country once played in the early childhood education movement. Even while recognizing that an overall evaluation of a diverse and complex educational system is difficult to make, it nonetheless appears that early childhood schooling in England suffers from adherence to a rather dated philosophy, insufficient facilities, and a general lack of excitement and experimentation. This conclusion is reached whether one evaluates early childhood schooling from a professional vantage point (curricula, program, facilities) or as an academic discipline (research and development). And it is all the more surprising when one considers the unique tradition of support of nursery education by the government, the innovation and change at the primary level in contemporary British education, and the heightened interest and activity in early childhood schooling in the United States.

In spite of some recent ameliorative efforts, an acute shortage of nursery school facilities exists in most parts of England. While various estimates are offered, most experts agree that fewer than 10 percent of children age 3 through 5 attend a preschool and only half that number are enrolled in schools that are prepared to provide educational experiences and enrichment.[2] Many of the early childhood facilities are inadequate with regard to space and equipment. In addition, a significant but not major proportion of assistant teachers have had no formal schooling beyond high school. Further, there are practically no provisions in most programs for children younger than 3 years of age. Although the facilities provided by the "urban programme"[3] are intended to increase the number of minority children receiving preschool experiences, the fact remains that for most advantaged and for most disadvantaged children alike, formal preschool education is simply unavailable.

The guiding philosophies, theories, and educational models of Pestalozzi, Froebel, and McMillan,[4] which focus on integrity, freedom, and opportunity for growth for the young child are still very evident and are reflected in the respect and care shown the children in English preschool centers.[5] What is also quite evident is the presence of psychoanalytic teachings and the concomitant absence of the influence of Montessori and Piaget and of any strong cognitive orientation. The implications of these theoretical positions are manifested in all phases of the nursery program, including teacher behavior, available materials, and curricular activities. In general, current practice in England does not yet reflect the influence of the recent attention and research devoted to cognitive development, effects of early stimulation and deprivation, language growth, and social reinforcement.[6]

In Great Britain, relatively little communication and collaboration takes place between psychologists and educators in the field of early childhood schooling. The division between these two groups is based on issues which are hardly new: basic research vs. field application. Both scientific activity and the advancement of early childhood schooling are hindered by this lack of unity.

Practically no research or experimentation is being carried out that is directly concerned with development and evaluation of curricula for the normal preschool child. The few recent investigations dealing with this age group that one encounters are usually concerned with compensatory education for minority and working-class children.[7] In this regard it may be pertinent to note that much of child development research in Great Britain is oriented toward special or deviant populations. For example, of the large faculty at the Institute of Education, University of London, responsible for research and instruction in child development, only a few individuals are carrying out research dealing with the "typical" child. This preoccupation with the exceptional child is undoubtedly influenced by government policy, which determines the allocation of research funds for different areas.

There always has been sympathy and support for early childhood programs in the government's Department of Education and Science. However, historically, and to a large extent currently, administrative responsibility for many educational activities for the child under 5 falls within the Ministry of Health, rather than the Department of Education and Science. Social reform rather than academe spawned the establishment of the earliest nursery schools in England, and the social-welfare orientation is still pervasive, at least in terms of government responsibility and administration. Indeed, one of the factors that appears to have sustained the relative inaction on behalf of preschool education is the implicit (though sometimes explicit) sentiment that nursery schools should be provided only for deprived children of working mothers, while children from middle-class homes should not be separated from their mothers. (Parenthetically, it may be noted that preschool education in the United States followed quite the reverse course—concern for the poor came considerably later than the early laboratory nursery schools of the university community.)

Although the 1944 Education Act gave local authorities the *power* to make provisions for children of nursery age, for various reasons it proved to have few tangible effects. Perhaps the influence of psychoanalytic biases, stressing the importance of the child's place at home with his mother, was an even stronger power. For whatever reason, some local authorities are extremely resistant to the development of preschool educational programs and fail to capitalize on available resources.

It remains true that the planning, responsibility, and stimulus for new movements in nursery schooling lie *less* within the province of the Department of Education and Science than do corresponding efforts in any other phase of education. Thus, the phenomenal growth of Pre-School Playgroups, the major development within nursery schooling of the last 20 years in Great Britain, occurred almost completely outside the jurisdiction of that Department. However, this form of preschool education, which is the only kind of nursery schooling serving middle-class groups that has expanded substantially, has recently received critical financial and professional support from the government.

In reviewing the status of early childhood schooling in England as well as the directions it seems to be taking, it must be remembered that this is a period of transition and change in educational practices in Great Britain as well as internationally. Consequently, our generalizations may have to be significantly modified in the future as changes occur in the degree and mode of educational support. It must be further recognized that the generalizations offered here represent motifs or central trends and that there are, of course, exceptions to the norm.

The report which follows is divided into 4 major sections. The first provides information on the procedures and data sources used in the study of current early childhood schooling programs in England. Section two describes the present-day organization of early childhood programs in the British system and summarizes the observations made of ongoing early childhood schooling programs. A third section outlines the major recommendations with respect to early childhood schooling in Britain of the Plowden Report of 1967, and a fourth reviews recent and ongoing research and development efforts of both direct and indirect import to early childhood education. We conclude with a summary of the above and a discussion of future potential.

PROCEDURES AND DATA SOURCES

The impressions and information pertaining to the practice and implementation of preschool education contained in this report were gathered during 2 visiting periods (Fall 1968 and Summer 1969). Although a variety of methods was used in our approach to the subject, the two most fruitful procedures for obtaining the data were interviews and direct observations.

Interviews More than 50 individuals were interviewed in the course of this survey. Included in the sample were members of the state and local departments of education responsible for advising and planning preschool programs. Also consulted were university faculty members from education and psychology departments and investigators directing research or special projects in early education. Personnel immediately involved in the administration of preschool education such as headmistresses, teachers, and nursery nurses were both interviewed and observed. Other respondents included the principal of a nursery nurses college, an author of a book on preschool education, a staff member of the Nursery School Association of Great Britain and Northern Ireland, and several members of the very active Pre-School Playgroup Association. Some 10 parents completed our diverse sample.

While the specific interview schedule varied with the structure of the situation and the role of the participant, the thrust of each interview, where possible, was directed toward the following interdependent issues:

1   The educational philosophy guiding preschool education
2   The nature of preschool curricula
3   The type, availability, and adequacy of facilities and programs available in different parts of England
4   The current status of preschool education in England
5   Future projections of the course of preschool education for the average child and for the disadvantaged child, locally and nationally

The information obtained during these interviews supplemented the data provided by the observations of nursery schools and nursery classes attached to regular Infant Schools.

Observations   More than 30 different nursery classes were visited in the course of this project. Every effort was made to include the varied types of preschool arrangements offered in England. Thus, visits were made to state-supported classes, privately run classes, university-affiliated nursery schools, and to cooperative or parent-administered facilities. Several day nurseries also were sampled. Some nursery classes were affiliated with or attached to regular Infant Schools, and some were conducted in separate nursery schools. Classes meeting for morning sessions, afternoon sessions, and all-day sessions were sampled in a comparable manner.

Schools selected for study were located for the most part in the cities of Bristol and London and in cities and towns in the counties of Greater London, Kent, Leicester, and Nottingham. Both urban and suburban schools were surveyed.

A minimum of 2½ hours was devoted to each visit. Some schools warranted longer periods of observation, especially the full-time state-supported nursery schools having several nursery classes on their premises. Each nursery class included for study was observed and appraised in terms of several different factors and dimensions. Initially these ratings were recorded in diary fashion, a method shortly supplanted by the use of an observation and interview schedule.[8] This schedule, entitled the |I|D|E|A| Guide to the Appraisal of Nursery Schools, provided greater structure, objective observation, and information than did the more anecdotal diary procedure and consequently served as the basis for the majority of observations and interviews.

The Observation and Interview Schedule   The observation and interview schedule (see Appendix A) used for studying English preschools was designed to facilitate the recording and organization of an observer's impressions of a nursery school. The schedule taps a number of critical areas relevant to the program, personnel, and organization of a preschool facility.

The first section of the instrument pertains to information gathered by direct observation and includes 12 different sets of categories. The first relates to the class or school structure and covers demographic factors pertinent to the children, school, and community, as well as information characterizing staff members, including their qualifications and training. Curricular content is listed in another category, and the frequency of use and degree to which the material and activity were regulated and structured are noted here. A separate list of basic materials and equipment appears under another grouping. The presence or absence of specific material and equipment, its quality and condition, as well as the degree of free selection of its use, also are evaluated.

Another part of the first section deals with more general issues and attempts to provide overall assessments of such factors as mood, atmosphere, attractiveness, comfort, discipline, teacher behavior, quality of interpersonal interactions, stimulation, and responsiveness. Answers to these molar questions were based on interview data as well as on observable events. The last 3 categories of this section provide an opportunity for more discursive comments and observations. Such general statements and anecdotal incidents proved to be a helpful complement to the more structured and objective aspects of the instrument.

The schedule's second part allows for the recording and organization of information derived from interviews conducted with personnel at the various sites that were visited. Conclusions apropos of the specific and overall curricular and program goals were verified and clarified in this context. Material germane to selection of children, parent activities, and staff training and responsibilities are also compiled and recorded here.

ORGANIZATION AND PRACTICE

Although a variety of types of preschool facilities may be found in Great Britain, only government-supported nursery schools and nursery

classes come under the aegis of the Department of Education and
Science. Nursery schooling has been an official part of England's educational system since the Education Act of Parliament in 1944. This
act was highly consistent with the earlier 1918 Education Act which
empowered local authorities to make nursery school arrangements for
children over 2 and under 5 for the purpose of enhancing children's
physical and mental development.[9]

At both the state and local level are inspectors responsible for
both preschool and Infant School conditions. These inspectors consult
and mediate between the authorities and school administrators and
teachers. The role of Her Majesty's Chief Inspector and of the local inspectors appears to be a salient one, and critical decisions regarding
policy and practice, but not budget, seem to be determined and imple-
mented through this line of communication.

Virtually all other major categories of preschools, such as the Pre-
School Playgroups, the day nurseries, and most private nursery schools,
fall outside the jurisdiction of the Department of Education. Although
educational goals are important for these organizations, the responsibility, administration, and inspection of these institutions are delegated
to the Ministry of Health. Both Pre-School Playgroups and day nurseries
are registered under the Day Nursery and Child Minders Act of 1948.

Nursery Schools and Nursery Classes

Table I presents the various types of nursery school establishments for
which the Department of Education and Science is responsible. The
majority of these come under two principal categories of publicly
supported facilities: separately maintained nursery schools and nursery
classes attached to infant and junior schools. In general, the nursery
school is housed on its own separate premises and usually comprises
several or more classes. The nursery class, as distinguished from a
nursery school, is attached to a regular Infant School and may be located in the same or an adjacent building. In all cases, whether nursery
class or nursery school, outdoor play space for preschool children is
not shared by older-age schoolmates.

Facilities   State nursery schools are housed in a wide variety of structures. Some are quite old and previously had been used for different
purposes, and others are quite modern and designed specifically for
use by young children.[10] However, a school located in converted facilities may occasionally benefit from bonus rooms, which might have

TABLE I ESTABLISHMENTS INSPECTED BY THE DEPARTMENT OF
EDUCATION IN ENGLAND. THE FIGURES RELATE TO JANUARY 1965.

Type of Establishment	Number	Children Age 2	Children Age 3	Children Age 4	Age 2–4
Nursery Schools	420	1,668	9,439	10,553	21,660
Nursery Classes in Primary Schools		171	7,349	167,419	174,939
Direct-Grant Nursery Schools	16	51	322	299	672
Recognized Independent Nursery Schools	9	39	131	106	276
Other Independent Nursery Schools	194	84	806	1,907	2,797
Recognized Independent Schools Other Than Nurseries		20	322	3,845	4,187
Other Independent Schools Other Than Nurseries		168	1,851	8,747	10,766
Total	639	2,201	20,220	192,876	215,297

These statistics are condensed from *Children and their Primary Schools,* Plowden Report, vol. 1, pp. 109–110.

originally been butler's pantries or dressing or serving rooms, and other unusual features, such as elaborate cupboards, bay windows, sunken floors, and raised platforms, which ordinarily would not be included in a nursery school structure. The use of converted buildings and the attachment of nursery school classes to Infant Schools provides an atmosphere of individuality and variability for the nursery school regime. The nursery school located in a crowded urban setting is matched by one situated on spacious grounds which often are used in imaginative and stimulating ways.

In view of the basic similarity in philosophy and activity between preschool facilities, whether a nursery school or a nursery class, there is a surprising degree of disagreement regarding the ideal location of nursery facilities. Teachers and headmistresses who direct programs in nursery schools prefer separate nursery schools rather than classes attached to Infant Schools and feel young children thrive more in a situation where they are not likely to feel overwhelmed by older children.

Teachers of nursery classes held in Infant Schools express the opposite preference. They feel that attendance at a nursery class on the same premises as the Infant School facilitates the child's transition to the older classes. Many headmistresses and teachers concur, since they feel this latter arrangement places nursery schooling in its proper educational context and reduces its social mission flavor.

In spite of the 1944 Education Act, expansion of nursery school facilities, especially new schools, has been extremely limited. However, since 1964, a number of nursery classes were opened to provide care for children of teachers returning to the classroom.[11] In most cases, these classes have admitted other children in the community as well. All existing nursery schools and classes have long waiting lists and operate a system of strict priorities sometimes based on geographic locale but often on grounds of family hardship, most often a combination of financial and medical problems.

The geographic location of government-supported nursery facilities throughout the country is haphazard and does not necessarily reflect the needs of any particular area with regard to the population age or the degree of neighborhood deprivation.[12] Children attending state-supported nurseries tend to be predominantly from working-class backgrounds, but children from middle-class and minority origins are also represented in these programs, their proportion varying with the location of a particular facility.

The proportion of minority and deprived children in nursery schools will increase appreciably as the Urban Programme unfolds during the next few years. With an initial budget of £3½ million, many new nursery schools and classes will be built in poorer neighborhoods and in urban areas considered to have the most acute social difficulties. Table II presents the distribution of the projected additions. The 2 major criteria for selection appear to be high population density and proportion of immigrant children on school rolls. The purpose of these new facilities is to provide help for children from deprived backgrounds in overcoming their "educational handicaps."[13]

This new development represents the first major extension of government-sponsored nursery schooling since World War II and could well serve as a catalyst for the early childhood schooling movement in England. Curricula may be rethought and revised to make them more consistent with the educational goals for this new sample of children. New programs and other advances will have to be evaluated and appraised. The issues of curriculum development and evaluation

TABLE II PROJECTIONS OF ADDITIONAL NURSERY SPACES FOR
1968 THROUGH 1972 AS PART OF THE NURSERY EDUCATION
PROVISION OF THE URBAN PROGRAMME

	New Schools	Newly Built Nursery Classes	Remodeled Schools	Full-time Places
Phase I	21	68	71	5,250
Phase II	43	97	85	5,376
Total	64	165	156	10,626

SOURCE: E. McDougall, Her Majesty's Chief Inspector for Infant and Nursery
Education, personal communication.

are likely to become salient ones and their impact felt in university
and nursery school circles alike.

Staffing Compared with most other nursery arrangements in Great
Britain,[14] nursery classes and nursery schools are most impressive in
terms of trained personnel, space, equipment, and program planning.
The head teacher, or headmistress, or supervising teacher, is usually a
woman of considerable education and training. She has either a college
degree or a teaching certificate from a 3-year teachers college.

The size of the staff varies with the size of the school. In larger
schools, with all-day programs for 50 to 120 children, there usually are
at least 3 or 4 additional staff members. Their qualifications and training range from those of qualified teachers, to assistants with a nursery
nurse's degree, to assistants without any special training in education.
The cook and the kitchen helpers are also an important part of the
school staff. A smaller school of 40 children might have a qualified
teacher and 2 assistants, one of whom is a nursery nurse. A nursery
class connected to an Infant School generally has an enrollment of 20
to 30 children with a trained teacher and 1 or 2 assistants.

Although the Department of Education and Science regulates
standards for staff qualifications (every school must have a trained
teacher at the helm) and for staff and student ratios (one trained
teacher and one nursery assistant for every 20 full-time children), each
school is allowed flexibility in the distribution of staff. This flexibility
permits preschools to develop different kinds of staff arrangements.

Many of the nursery assistants in the state-run classes are nursery
nurses, products of a specially run, 2-year training program which pre-
pares candidates to work with young children. This program heavily
stresses practicum training, and students spend half their time in the

classroom and the remainder in schools and nurseries. Most of the nursery nurses receive this training prior to completion of secondary school and receive a nursery nurse's degree.[15] The nursery nurses, both student and graduate, observed in the course of this study were attractive, competent, warm, friendly, and loving to children. Apparently, candidates are screened with regard to certain personal characteristics as well as academic qualifications. Their intensive training in educational practice, child development, health, nutrition, and other subjects reinforces their initial potential and produces an excellent person to work with children.

However, the high proportion of nursery nurses and other types of ancillary staff reflects the shortage of trained teachers at this educational level and also suggests a limited budget for educational services for this age group. It is also clear that the continued use of ancillary help and nursery nurses is anticipated for future programs as well.[16] In the current programs, where the primary focus is on play, self-selection of materials, and emotional development, and where no direct tuition of children is involved, the use of a high proportion of ancillary staff presents few problems. If, however, curricular goals begin to include more complex educational objectives relative to acquisition of language and other cognitive skills, a more professional background may be required. At any rate, the vocational program for training nursery nurses appears to be extremely useful and should be carefully studied by educational planners in the United States.

Curricula: Content and Practice   At the present time, the major curriculum emphasis of the British nursery program leans heavily toward the social-emotional goals of the traditional nursery school.[17] The guiding philosophy is to provide children the opportunity for play and social companionship of peers so that they may develop their maximum powers and potential. Nursery school is a place where the child's needs for security, activity, space, and social contact are to be satisfied.[18] Children who attend the government-supported facilities, by and large, do indeed have the opportunity to engage in play in spacious circumstances and are exposed to appropriate play material in the context of companions and skilled leadership. Play and free selection of activities is the predominant pattern. Most teachers feel that structuring a child's program in nursery school prevents his natural curiosity from evolving and being satisfied.

The following sequence of activities might occur during an ordinary day for a child attending a full-day session. He arrives at school some time between 9:00 and 10:00 A.M., although the nursery session might actually begin at 9:00 or slightly earlier. The children are not expected to arrive all at the same time. In fact, variability in arrival time sometimes is encouraged by the headmistress to allow her the opportunity to greet personally each child and parent. This same pattern is repeated at departure, some younger or immature children leaving at 2:30 while others stay as late as 3:30 P.M.

If the child has been recently enrolled in the school, the mother is allowed and encouraged to spend the day with him. At most schools, children are gradually separated from their mothers, and, while individual differences in attitudes do exist among supervising teachers, this gradual weaning of mother and child seems to be an extremely prevalent practice. Some children may require their mother's presence for only a day or two, while for other children the separation process may take weeks. This permissiveness and flexibility regarding separation come in sharp contrast to private schools in England and the United States where parents usually are unwelcome. The teachers we observed tended to be warm and related to parents as well as to children and proved to be highly informed about the child's entire family.

If our hypothetical child is attending a large nursery school, he might now join a group of children his own age. More likely, and especially if he is in a class attached to a regular Infant School, the age of his peers will range from 3 to 5, being mostly 4 and 5. As a rule, our child will engage in active play for approximately the first two hours of a school morning. If the weather is good, not a highly probable event, the child has access to the outdoors where he or she can engage in water play, climbing activities, or tricycle riding. Water play is much more in evidence in England than in the US, both indoors and outdoors. Climbing apparatus is to be found indoors as well as outdoors and is abundantly used. Tricycles and other wheel toys are limited in number but are much in demand. A surprising fact is the frequent absence of outdoor swings. Very often, when questioned about this, the teacher would produce one or two swings from a storage closet. It was difficult to determine precisely why there was not greater use of this type of equipment. Perhaps the need to assemble and dismantle swings each time they are used, along with the generally inclement weather, may have been a deterrent.

If the child from preference or necessity spends the morning indoors, he can choose from a number of activities. He can build with blocks, spend time in the Wendy house (doll house) and doll corner, play in the hospital corner (a play theme almost nonexistent in US nursery schools), play with water, and engage in sand play (there is more indoor sand activity here than outdoor sand activity). A variety of graphic art materials is available to tempt the child. Some days, he is busy with easel painting and crayons, other days with finger painting.

Additional equipment available in most schools most days is clay, dress-up clothes, housekeeping materials, puppets, puzzles, books, science materials (including plants and animals), and trucks. British nurseries tend to utilize more improvised toys and implements than do their American counterparts. The separate nursery schools generally have more play materials and equipment than do nursery classes attached to Infant Schools. (However, some of the nursery classes visited had been in existence for only 2 or 3 years.) Another obvious difference between nursery schools and nursery classes is the presence of materials relevant to the 3 R's. In nursery classes, bulletin boards frequently have posted material, pictures and words, relating directly to academic goals of language, math, and science curricula. This is rarely observed in a regular nursery school. In the main, though, nursery schools and nursery classes draw upon the same philosophy and focus on similar educational objectives.

As the morning approaches the lunch hour, our child is rounded up, toileted, and may next listen to a story or participate in simple rhythms. Then he proceeds to a formal lunch period. From the age of admission to a nursery school children are expected to eat very properly—and every effort is made to assist them in this accomplishment. The product of this tutoring is the exemplary manners the children display while consuming the well-balanced and nourishing meal that is provided.

Following lunch comes a nap. These naps, frequently taken outdoors in cots, occasionally in rather incredible weather, are no doubt a residual practice of the first open-air nursery schools in England. After a long nap for the child who needs it, there might be some further play, and then home.

Schools on half-day sessions usually do not serve lunch. Historically, most state nursery facilities were run on all-day programs with the midday meal assuming major importance because of its nutritional value and because it offered a means of establishing good social habits. In 1953, schools operating on half-day sessions and enrolling twice as many children were opened on an experimental basis.[19] Observation and teacher reports indicated that the results of these experimental efforts were highly positive, and half-day nursery sessions have now achieved formal approval even though lunch may be omitted. However, in most state nursery schools, a majority of the children still attend the all-day program while a small proportion of children attend either a morning or an afternoon session.

Official policy, as expressed in and influenced by the Plowden Report,[20] favors half-day sessions for middle-class children while still recommending all-day sessions for children from needy families. The latter tend to be more characteristic of the separate nursery school while nursery classes attached to Infant Schools appear to offer more half-day programs. As expansion of nursery schooling comes to include more middle-class children and as the nursery class rather than the nursery school becomes the model and modal arrangement, it is anticipated that the number of half-day sessions will increase.

Aside from minor differences, the program and philosophy of the all-day program are parallel to those of the part-time program. Since lunch is omitted, the milk snack, a casual affair for the all-day child, becomes a more structured routine for the half-day child. Morning and afternoon sessions are similar, with the latter often including a longer rest period or nap.

The child we have been following might have had a quite similar day at many nursery schools in the United States. One important difference, however, is the degree to which the teacher intercedes in and supervises the children's play. The teacher, so clearly visible in the vicinity of swings, climbing apparatus, and carpentry area in the American nursery school, is not in evidence in this same supervisory fashion in the British preschool. British teachers view themselves as a resource, available to the child when the latter expresses a need, and in teacher-child interactions it is usually the child who initiates the contact. British children are allowed and expected to be independent, and one consequence of this approach is the greater freedom the children seem to enjoy. This is especially apparent in children's minor altercations. Teachers almost never interfere in these outbursts, and children rarely expect or ask them to do so, apparently resulting in little tattling and whining behavior. It is only in the more structured context of story-telling, rhythms, and dining that adults assume a more active and stimulating role. A child attending a half-day nursery program encounters less frequent direct teacher-child interactions, since lunch is not usually served at schools which are predominantly on half-day schedules.

Another important difference between English and American preschools is the greater role which cognitive goals and activities have assumed in American preschool curricula, especially in recent years. From the interviews and observations made at English institutions, it appears that headmistresses and teachers do not perceive the nursery school experience as primarily directed toward the manipulation of the intellectual and language repertoire of the children. Nursery school is seen as the place where children from small apartments, with restricted play areas, can play freely with peers and have a balanced hot lunch.

The saga of the effects of early intellectual stimulation on later cognitive development has not infiltrated the domain of the average British-trained nursery school teacher. Consequently, the importance and potential of stimulation and intervention at this early age level are not recognized in this teacher group. Intellectual consequences of attending nursery schools in England seem to be fortuitous by-products and not functionally derived from planned curricula. In fact, many teachers appear to be hostile to such concepts as cognition, stimulation, intervention, and modification, and to the materials and approach of Montessori. Although there are two Montessori School training centers in London, their past influence has been greatly limited, there being little communication and understanding of the Montessori program objectives and methods.

The inventive materials now inundating the more innovative British Infant School appear to be virtually nonexistent in the nursery school. Although important and beneficial nursery practices have infiltrated the Infant School, it appears that the positive educational influences of the latter have not operated downward. One slight change in attitude was noted in the interviews of our second as contrasted with our first visit. Teachers were less hostile to questions regarding cognitive training and sometimes spontaneously raised these issues themselves. However, no change was noted in practice.

One wonders if efforts equal to those devoted to the development of good table manners were directed to language training whether the "working class" speech of many of the children would be modified. Language and language training would appear to have special significance in Great Britain since language type is so frequently correlated with an individual's position in the British social structure. However, there is no indication that in the near future working-class children in England will be exposed to deliberate language training in nursery schools.

The vocabulary and concepts of Piaget, so salient in the Infant School,[21] were not verbalized in any of the discussions with nursery headmistresses and teachers. Teachers by and large confuse programs of cognitive stimulation with achievement training. Basically, they disapprove of anything that suggests direct stimulation or training since their orientation is the independent unfolding of the child's potential. A further observation, indicative of the stereotyped aspect of the conventional curriculum, was the similarity and lack of variability of nursery programs from one school to another. A program structure characteristic of one state nursery school was frequently reflective of most other programs.

Day Nurseries

Table III indicates the various preschool facilities under the jurisdiction of the Ministry of Health (excluding Pre-School Playgroups). Local Authority Day Nurseries constitute an important set of facilities regulated outside the Department of Education. Their major growth occurred during World War II when they were established to care for children whose mothers were working in factories and at other defense-related efforts. After the war, except for a short temporary period, their number fell sharply, as part of a deliberate policy of the Ministries of Health and Education. In general, the Ministry of Health, historically hostile to the separation of the child under 5 from his or her mother, views these nurseries as justified only for children in special need on the basis of health or social grounds.[22]

TABLE III   ESTABLISHMENTS FOR WHICH THE MINISTRY OF HEALTH IS RESPONSIBLE IN ENGLAND. THE FIGURES RELATE TO DECEMBER 1965

Type of Establishment or Provision	Number	Number of Children or Places
Local Health Authority nurseries	448	16,470
Private nurseries run by factories	56	2,098
Other private nurseries	2,108	50,950
Child-minders retained by Local Health Authorities	865	1,482
Registered daily minders	3,347	(not available)

(These statistics are condensed from *Children and Their Primary Schools,* Plowden Report, vol. 1, pp. 109–110.)

Thus, while the organized impetus for these institutions came from industrial pressures, they are now operated as a social service mostly for the children of unsupported mothers. It should be noted that these nurseries hardly provide a sufficient number of places for eligible children, and all have a waiting list. Most provide full-day rather than part-time care for children under the age of 5. Children under 2 are also included in this facility. Although the type of physical care afforded is of the highest order, the educational program, curricula, and trained nursery staff are, in general, below the standards of other types of preschools, a state of affairs reflecting the purpose and support of these schools.

Most of the supervisory staff have received their training in health rather than in education. There is relatively little concern with pre-school programs. However, toys, books, dolls, and stuffed animals are available. Art materials and creative activity come into play more sporadically and only at specified times. One gets the feeling that children are milling about, marking time, waiting—a not dissimilar feeling from that conveyed by the atmosphere of many day-care centers in the United States. In general, the younger 2-year-olds tend to segregate themselves from the 3-to-5-year-old children. Finally, there are no active programs relating to the participation and education of mothers.

Pre-School Playgroups

Pre-School Playgroups, akin to cooperative nursery schools in the United States, are organized, supported, and jointly run by parents to care for each other's children and have been in operation in Great Britain since World War II. The Save the Children Fund pioneered the original organization of playgroups, especially for underprivileged children. In the early period of development of these preschool groups, a variety of other playgroups were initiated by some voluntary organizations. However, the rapid expansion of this type of institution has occurred in connection with the Pre-School Playgroups Association (PPA), which helped organize more than 1,500 groups during the 5-year period between 1963 and 1968.[23]

Since each Pre-School Playgroup is spontaneously formed by parents, with occasional help from the PPA organization, there is considerable variability from group to group with regard to size, facilities, program, and the training and education of the supervisor in charge. With the growth of the PPA as an organization and the mushrooming

of Pre-School Playgroups, standards and regulations are now developing which will lead to greater uniformity.[24]

Since most of the PPA groups are self-supporting (occasionally
the local authorities will contribute a small sum), a nominal fee is
charged to cover expenses for salaries, rent, equipment, and other
materials. As a rule, the school day is limited to a morning or afternoon
session and, while the sample is predominantly aged 3 through 5,
some younger children are included. Most playgroups have only one
class, comprising children of varying ages. Few children attend 5 sessions a week, the modal frequency being 2 to 3.

The average day is divided into 3 periods: free play with access to
a variety of materials and equipment, juice time and routines (toileting
and washup), and a "community" experience such as storytelling or
singing. Creative and play equipage such as sand, paints and crayons,
blocks, puzzles, and books are very much in evidence. The low frequency of water and clay is probably a function of small quarters.
Pianos are rarely seen and, in general, there is a very small amount of
musical play and activity. Since most children attend for only a half-
day session, naps and resting are rarely encountered. There is no evidence of formal academic activity (numbers and letters), but science
and nature corners are in abundance. Aside from the less frequent degree of musical activity and the reduced emphasis on routines, partially
a consequence of the half-day session, curricular activity and materials
are essentially a more modest version of the program in the state
nursery schools.[25]

Parents most often enroll their children in a Pre-School Playgroup
after first exploring alternatives in their immediate and adjacent neighborhoods. A Pre-School Playgroup is rarely a parent's first choice but
is selected when other facilities and programs are totally absent or
markedly inadequate. However, parental reactions to the program are
highly positive. Their satisfaction and gratitude are in marked contrast
to parent reactions to private nursery schools. For example, not one
PPA parent voiced any complaint during the many interviews that were
conducted, while many parents with children in private nursery schools
expressed reservation about sending their children to nursery school.
The major criticism and a source of conflict they noted was the feeling
that excessive control was being exercised in the private nurseries.
Pre-School Playgroup parents did not experience this conflict and
seemed pleased that they and their children had access to this type
of group experience.

Initially, Pre-School Playgroup parents were predominantly middle class, with the more established middle class providing the leadership and assistance to the emerging middle-class populations. Recently, however, classes have been started in a number of working-class areas. The problem of housing these groups (frequently operated out of members' homes) is even more acute in these areas. Barracks, club-rooms, almshouses, church halls, community centers, Further Education Centers, athletic clubs, and a variety of other premises have been used. Although government-built, -operated, and -supported housing is constantly being constructed, it is only very rarely that space is afforded to PPA groups.

Although Pre-School Playgroups fall under the jurisdiction of the Ministry of Health, other national and local educational authorities supply financial and professional help. For example, the Inner London Education Authority pays for two organizers for the PPA, and the Department of Education and Science has made a 3-year grant to the PPA to pay for a national advisor who assists in the formation of new groups. In addition, the Department of Education and Science conducts courses for supervisors and parent participants. Also, through a recent measure, both Pre-School Playgroups and day nurseries now share a budget allocation of £150 thousand made available as part of the Urban Programme.

The role of the parent is highly salient in the PPA. Although, in general, the British tend to be cognizant of parental concerns in preschool education, nowhere is it reflected more clearly than in this organization. Parents initiate, plan, and participate as teachers in the playgroups of their own children and serve as advisors of groups outside their community as well without any remuneration and frequently at their own expense. Parental education and participation is an avowed purpose of the PPA, and the outlet which it provides for mothers no doubt partially explains its phenomenal growth. In 1968, more than 100,000 children were attending an estimated 3,000 playgroups.

The attention paid mothers, and the opportunities it provides them, points up an important distinction in objectives between this type of arrangement and the state and private nursery schools. However, the rapid development of the preschool movement in the past, and the even greater growth anticipated in the future, cannot be completely accounted for in terms of parental rewards and satisfactions. The burgeoning of these groups must be viewed as the response of the citizenry to fill a void existing at this educational level. Parents want to send their children to nursery school for educational purposes, for social purposes, for personal purposes, and desperately search for any means to do so.

What, then, are the limitations of this movement which involves the community, generates enthusiasm among mothers, and provides spaces for their children? Response to this question raises fundamental issues regarding the philosophy and purpose of preschool education. The particular Pre-School Playgroups observed during the course of our survey were uniformly disappointing and even depressing, even though they were recommended as especially exemplary. Equipment, toileting facilities, and other materials were considerably below standard, and the housing facilities were often cramped and inadequate. Although it has been estimated that, as a rule, two-thirds of the staff are professionally trained,[26] this contention is not supported by the observations of this survey. The supervisor of the unit was more often a graduate of a nursery nurses college than a trained teacher. Many Pre-School Playgroups have only enlightened mothers in the supervisory role, with a health nurse providing occasional help. Adult-to-child ratio was much more satisfactory than the trained-staff-to-child ratio; the recommended staff arrangement of 3 to 4 adults to 18 to 30 children was observed.[27]

In view of the limitations of trained staff, facilities, and, often, programs, one must reluctantly conclude that, while these facilities are better than none at all, they can hardly be viewed as representing the potential best in preschool education. If nursery schooling is to be considered educational in purpose rather than as a baby-sitting enterprise, then preschool groups in their present form should be interpreted as a stopgap procedure merely and not as a solution to the needs of early childhood schooling. Nevertheless, since at present no other program is projected that will markedly alleviate the shortage of nursery places for middle-class children, one can expect an even greater expansion of Pre-School Playgroups. It is this writer's opinion that the ultimate contribution of this movement toward the education of children and to the growth of early childhood schooling in Great Britain will be a function of the degree to which supervision and support are provided by the Department of Education.

Private Nursery Schools

As Tables I and III indicate, the regulation of most private nursery schools falls outside the province of the Department of Education and

Science. Although private facilities have increased rapidly since World War II, the population accommodated represents only a small fraction of the children enrolled in nursery school. Nevertheless, children between the ages of 2 through 5 do attend private nursery schools, nursery classes in small private primary schools, and nursery schools operated by factories and hospitals. The ensuing discussion of private nursery facilities does not include references to those maintained by factories and hospitals, since this type of facility was not observed in the study.

Generally speaking, the small private nursery schools are attended by suburban middle-class children and the nursery classes in private primary schools are attended by urban upper-middle-class children whose parents can afford the fee. In staffing, physical facilities, space, and equipment, they are generally superior to the Pre-School Playgroups and markedly inferior to state nursery schools. Although the nursery class is usually assigned only one room, the children have access to the outdoor and dining space of the rest of the school.

Curricula and program are typically quite formal and highly structured. Children are expected to sit in their seats for periods of time which seem to be too restrictive and demanding for the average preschool child. The informality, choice, and spontaneity common in most state nursery schools and the more innovative Infant Schools are frequently absent. A considerable amount of time is spent in developing appropriate manners, behavior controls, and academic skills. Simple achievement skills rather than cognitive growth and development appear to be the program's educational objectives. The mode and style of teaching observed often was rather rigid.

The parents interviewed who had availed themselves of this type of facility seemed almost uniformly regretful that they had done so. The quality of private nursery schools in England has not mirrored the educational adequacy of similar institutions in the United States. The expansion of private nursery schools in England should be interpreted in the special context of the acute shortage of nursery school places in Great Britain.

Other Facilities and Resources

There are other types of facilities and resources in Great Britain which, although not directly involved in early childhood education, do have consequences for the psychosocial development of the preschool child and thus warrant some comment. Perhaps the most important of these is the *health nurse*. Financed by the Ministry of Health, she provides a link between the mother of the newborn child and the pertinent information and programs available at a governmental level. The health nurse makes regular visits to the home and may act as a consultant to the mother on matters concerning the child's emotional and social development as well as the child's physical health and growth. She performs a very important role and should be considered in any program which aims at facilitating early educational objectives by means of instruction of the young mother.

In addition to government-supported day nurseries, a number of private child-care facilities are available to the working mother. One is the *child minder,* who is registered, but not well-regulated, by the state and looks after babies for a fee. A related but larger and more organized institution for taking care of the infants of working mothers for a full day is the *Creche,* a concept which first arose in France and then spread to England. Of historical note is the fact that the first day nurseries in England were modeled after the Creche. The Creche is not oriented to educational goals, nor is it subject to close governmental supervision and regulation. Its orientation is basically medical, and staff members are usually nurses who are not educationally trained. It accepts babies as young as 1 month and, in general, is utilized by parents whose children are too young to attend a regular nursery class.

Finally, some note should be made of the Adventure Playgrounds, which are play areas that have been constructed in locations not originally intended for this purpose (e.g., vacant lots and rooftops).[28] Materials such as bricks, sand, wood, and discarded objects are made available for the child to use in a creative, imaginative manner. These unusual and creative play centers function as a neighborhood resource that is occasionally used by the preschool child but not, as a rule, by preschool programs.

THE PLOWDEN REPORT

In 1967, the Central Advisory Council of England, under the chairmanship of Lady Plowden, published a two-volume report entitled *Children and Their Primary Schools.* This report was the outgrowth of a 4-year study aimed at considering all aspects of primary education. The conditions and needs of education preceding compulsory schooling were also assessed and considered by the Council and were included in the final report.

The Plowden Report contains a number of specific recommendations with respect to early childhood schooling (see Appendix B). The primary recommendation is for the immediate expansion of nursery provisions in England, with the ultimate goal of making nursery schooling available by the late 1970s to all children from the age of 3 until the age of compulsory schooling. However, in reaffirmation of British tradition, the concept and merit of the nursery school as an adjunct to and not as a replacement for the home are clearly reflected in the Report. Thus, the recommendation for expansion contains the proviso that the majority of children should attend on only a part-time basis "because young children should not be separated for long from their mothers." The report does acknowledge that full-time nursery schooling must be available for a minority of children with special needs, estimated to be approximately 15 percent of all children from 3 through 5 years of age. It is recommended that children whose mothers cannot satisfactorily demonstrate to the authorities that they have exceptionally good reasons for working should receive low priority for all-day nursery places.

Further, the report recommends that all existing state-supported facilities for children from 3 through 5 should include educational components in their programs and should come under the jurisdiction of the Department of Education and local educational authorities. This proposal recognizes that the structure of the day nurseries, currently supervised by the Ministry of Health, will eventually change. The Council's emphasis on education is not intended to lessen concern for the physical well-being of children; rather, the report notes the positive potential of health and education officials working in concert with respect to programs for young children.

The report also attends to the more technical aspects of expanded nursery education. It advises, for example, that all nursery groups be under the ultimate supervision of a qualified teacher in a ratio of 1 teacher for every 60 children; in addition, all groups should include a trained nursery assistant for every 10 children. Nursery classes attached to Infant Schools are to be considered a regular part of those schools.

Although these recommendations indicate an immediate problem of staffing, the report includes suggestions for meeting the immediate needs of expanded nursery schooling through the utilization of existing nursery and primary school staffs. These suggestions are made feasible through additional recommendations which would delay the age of compulsory schooling and also limit the admittance dates of Infant Schools to once a year. (Children are currently admitted at the age of 5 at intervals of 4 months.) The problem of facilities to house new nursery groups is also dealt with in the report, with concern for immediate needs handled in a manner similar to that of staffing.

Joint planning of all services for young children, including nursery schooling, is recommended with the additional suggestion that attempts be made to locate service facilities close to both the children's homes and the primary schools. Until sufficient places are available, local educational authorities should be empowered and encouraged to give financial and other assistance to volunteer and other nonprofit groups which they consider capable of providing such services. These groups, with or without financial assistance, should be subject to inspection by the local educational authorities and the Department of Education.

The significance of early compensatory training for children from economically deprived backgrounds, for children with language difficulties, and for children with potential learning difficulties was emphasized. The recent expansion of nursery provision as part of the Urban Programme may be directly linked to this serious and impressive report which recommended that expansion of nursery schooling be considered an educational priority area demanding immediate efforts. It is of special interest to note that early childhood schooling was dealt with in relation to succeeding primary schooling. So often, these phases of schooling are treated so separately that any sense of a relationship between the two is lost. The so-called Plowden Report was particularly influential in its stimulation of the British Infant Schools, of much recent interest in the United States and elsewhere. Anything resembling a similar stimulation at the level of practice in early childhood schooling per se has not yet occurred.

RESEARCH

The amount of ongoing and recent research in Great Britain related to early childhood education encountered in the course of this survey proved to be rather limited. It is possible, of course, that certain relevant research may have been overlooked. However, particular effort was made to survey those centers and individuals likely to be engaged in research in this area, including a review of a conference on research by British investigators on early childhood development sponsored by the Centre for Advanced Studies in the Developmental Sciences. In addition, discussions with leading investigators confirmed the impression of a dearth of research effort on problems directly pertinent to preschool and early primary school education.

With a few important exceptions, the research activity that was scrutinized was disappointing. The majority of the studies provide little novelty in the way of procedures, approach, or theory. In general, the research tends to be atheoretical and almost completely isolated from related research and contemporary theoretical developments. For example, the work of Piaget, whose influence is very clearly evident in curricular development in Great Britain at the primary level,[29] is virtually ignored in research and thinking at the preschool level. Also disappointing is the failure of investigators to explore and capitalize upon those special cultural features which are indigenous to Great Britain. As examples, one can cite the diversity of cultural differences in language and customs extant among England, Scotland, Wales, and Northern Ireland, and the perhaps even greater diversity present among the many ethnic groups grossly categorized as "immigrants" (Cypriots, Pakistani, Africans, Orientals, etc.). Similarly, the rapidly expanding Pre-School Playgroups, with their manifold potential effects upon the child and the parent, offer unique opportunities for comparative study.

Since research in Great Britain at the primary and secondary school levels has in fact examined the educational consequences of ethnic and social class distinctions, one may expect that, in time, these issues will be reflected in educationally oriented research at the preschool level. Lively interest is already ongoing in the longitudinal effects of early emotional deprivation, separation of child from parent, and institutionalization. Whereas much of the initial work, stimulated by Bowlby's pioneering studies of maternal care and mental health,[30] was concerned with the detrimental effects of emotional deprivation upon emotional and social development, more recent investigators have emphasized the negative consequences for cognitive growth. Thus, M. L. Kellmer Pringle, director of the National Bureau for Cooperation in Child Care, has carried out a series of studies examining the effects of residential treatment and care upon language development, reading, and other intellectual achievements.[31] This tradition of research interest in early deprivation, coupled with the innovative theoretical and empirical work of such investigators as Bernstein[32] and Lawton[33] on social class differences in language style, provide a ready framework for the development of an investigative program on problems more specifically related to early childhood schooling.

A more detailed picture of research activities in Great Britain bearing on problems of early childhood schooling is next presented in two parts. The first covers investigations directly concerned with issues in early childhood schooling as well as research less proximal to the primary interest but with procedures and findings very relevant to preschool education. The second section summarizes studies in early childhood development which bear more indirectly on early childhood schooling issues.

Research Highly Relevant to Early Childhood Schooling Of all the research reviewed, the project currently being conducted in the Slough area under the leadership of W. H. L. Williams,[34] of the National Foundation for Educational Research, is most directly relevant to preschool educational issues. The objective of this project is to develop and evaluate a compensatory program for preschool children from relatively disadvantaged backgrounds. Slough, a working-class, industrial town located just west of London, affords an appropriate population for this purpose. A number of preschools in Slough were originally child-care centers that gradually developed into nursery schools. These offer an excellent opportunity for the introduction of new experimental programs. Starting with 30 children, the project eventually will involve 300, drawn from 5 nursery schools. The experimental program provides an enriched curriculum, emphasizing language and perceptual-motor skills. Longitudinal follow-up studies, including comparisons with control groups not exposed to the experimental curricula, are planned. The Peabody Picture Vocabulary, the Preschool Inventory, and several visual-motor tasks are among the procedures to be used in evaluating the effectiveness of the experimental programs. It is hoped that this project may eventually serve as a model for intervention programs in other nursery schools.

C. E. Gittins, at the University College of Swansea, is engaged in a similar undertaking in South Wales for children at the Infant School level.[35] In addition to the age of the children, Gittins' project differs from the one at Slough in that emphasis is placed primarily upon the development of curricular materials and programs that are appropriate to working-class children.

In relating the work at Slough and Swansea to experimental programs in the United States, it should be noted that the British working-class population is not comparable with the disadvantaged populations of the inner cities of the United States to which the Headstart Program, for example, has been largely directed.[36] In the case of the English working-class population, family structure is relatively intact, and level of income is stable. Thus, with respect to indices of social disorganization, the English working class is more comparable with the skilled industrial class in the United States. However, profound behavioral distinctions are associated with class membership in Great Britain that are comparable in certain respects with minority group membership in the United States. The distinctive language and behavioral style of the lower-class child stamps his place in the British social structure with almost the same force as color fixes the mobility of the black child in the American social structure. British research with older age groups suggests that "working class" language not only serves to identify the child's social status but also reinforces a particular value structure and fosters a restricted mode of interaction with the environment.

Noteworthy in this regard are the studies of the educational implications of linguistic usage and training carried out by B. Bernstein and associates at the Sociological Research Unit at the University of London Institute of Education.[37] Most of the children involved in the Bernstein investigations have been at the kindergarten or early primary level, but the research has significance for preschool education. One of Bernstein's major interests is the process through which social structure generates linguistic styles which then function to "transmit the culture and so constrain the behavior."[38] He has demonstrated systematic social class differences in flexibility, openness, and abstractness of language style, and has then attempted to link these differences to type of parent-child interaction and to the role system characterizing the family structure. In this connection, he has carried out detailed interviews with the mothers, investigating their response to educational opportunities, their preparation of the child for school, and their concepts of "brightness" and the functions of school.

The Bernstein group also has explored sex differences on cognitive measures and has examined identification with the teacher as a function of the child's sex. They have found such sex differences before the age of 6, boys manifesting more ambivalence than girls toward a female teacher. They also have carried out studies of the "answering" behavior of first-grade children and have linked the type of answer with the syntax of the question. A related analysis was made of the response of mother and child to the same question. In these and other linguistic studies, the Bernstein group has reported evidence indicating that the middle class employs a more "elaborate" coding system than does the working class, who tend to rely on a "restricted" syntax. They have further suggested that the differences in linguistic styles are linked to differences in child orientation, the middle-class parent being more likely to take into account the child's needs in his verbal interactions with the child.

Although most of Bernstein's work has been concerned with an analysis of structure and ongoing process rather than preparation for change, he also has carried out "training" studies.[39] In one recently completed project, children from 5 to 7 were given special linguistic training for three 20-minute sessions a week over a 2-year period. Although evidence of significant changes in the experimental group in comparison to the control group was obtained, Bernstein was more impressed with the difficulties of carrying out controlled experiments in a field setting, particularly with the extent to which uncontrolled variables such as teacher attitude and behavior may have influenced the results.

The ongoing and contrasting approaches to the significance of preschool experiences are provided by the experiment carried out by Donaldson and Wells at the University of Edinburgh[40] and by that of Connolly at the University of Sheffield.[41] Donaldson and Wells are investigating, by means of a longitudinal design, the effects of "experimental intervention" on the development of a wide range of cognitive and linguistic skills in a sample of 15 preschoolers between the ages of 3½ and 5. In lieu of experimental variation, Connolly plans to assess the effects of existing differences in preschool programs through comparisons of behavior of children in nursery schools, day nurseries, and children's institutions. A methodological problem which is also an objective of this study is to separate the influence of home background from that of various features of the nursery school environment. The methodology employed by Connolly is basically similar to that used by Pringle and her colleagues in their studies of cognitive development in deprived children.[42] Although the Pringle research has largely dealt with older age groups, some of the studies have been devoted to speech development at the nursery school level.

Research Secondarily Relevant to Early Childhood Schooling A number of other investigators are interested in linguistic behavior and language development, but their studies tend to be more psychological and less clearly linked to educational programs and outcomes. Thus Reynell, at the University of London, is constructing normative scales for the assessment of language development between the ages of 6 months and 6 years.[43] Ryan, at Cambridge, is engaged in a study comparing language development in severely subnormal individuals with that of nursery school children of equivalent mental age.[44] Mittler, at the University of Manchester, has reported that, at the age of 4, twins show a retardation in language when compared with children who are singletons.[45]

Several studies are currently underway dealing with cognitive processes, apart from language behavior, in preschool and elementary-age children. These tend to be concerned with developmental differences between normal and abnormal groups and only indirectly relate to educational matters. A prototype of this kind of project is that of Bryant, at Oxford, who recently has completed an investigation of age-related changes in learning strategies in 500 normal and severely subnormal children whose mental ages varied from 4 to 8.[46] The work entailed the use of simple discrimination and transfer tasks. Also in this general category are Barrett's study of information processing and short-term memory in normal and slow-learning children which was done at the University of Bristol,[47] and Woodward's investigations of noncognitive aspects of problem solving in children aged 5 to 9, with and without learning difficulties, carried out at the University College of Swansea.[48] Woodward also has done research on visual scanning and response time in the problem-solving behavior of subnormal children and a comparison group of normal children drawn from nursery schools and playgrounds. Clarke's work at the University of Hull investigating the development of equivalence relations in transfer situations in children varying in age from 3 to 5 is also important here.[49]

Other researchers are concerned with the effects of socialization practices and other early-experience variables upon the subsequent development of the child. John and Elizabeth Newson, at the University of Nottingham, have been particularly active in this area. Portions of their extensive research project, entailing a longitudinal study of children tested at their first, fourth, seventh, and, ultimately, eleventh year, bear upon educational issues.[50] For example, through one of their studies, they plan to analyze various forms of linguistic expression (e.g., storytelling, poetry, descriptive writing) in a 9- to 11-year-old sample and relate these measures to prior preschool verbal behavior and to other linguistic and verbal indices such as early exposure to storytelling, book ownership, and mother's encouragement of conversation. The Newsons also will explore the relationship between early measures of temperament and measures of subsequent linguistic expressions.[51]

Hindley, at the Child Development Centre, University of London, is another active investigator interested in developmental issues. Part of his research effort is directed at tracing the relationship between early abilities and subsequent intellectual performance in children tested at 6 and 18 months, and at 3, 5, 8, and 11 years of age. These studies should provide informative data on the role of early experiential as well as dispositional factors in subsequent intellectual performance.[52]

Commentary: Research and Practice   Research and practice are interdependent activities. Research influences practice, although at times there is a disturbing lag between research findings, their dissemination, and their utilization. Research, however, also follows practice, reflecting the emphasis which the culture places on particular social needs. Thus, a correlation obtains between the paucity of research on early childhood schooling and the relatively low priority which early childhood schooling holds in the British educational structure. The relationship between research and practice is also manifested at a theoretical level, most notably in that relatively little British research or practice concerned with the early age level is dependent upon the theoretical models provided by Montessori, by Piaget, and by social-learning theory.

Consequently, a substantial gap is to be found between British preschool practices and the implications of theory and empirical research on early stimulation and cognitive training currently salient in the United States. This situation is likely to change with the expansion by the British government of its nursery provision. As the national commitment becomes more substantial, a greater interest in alternative models will arise. Several previous evaluations have been made by British investigators of the influence and educational advantages of nursery school. Evidence from these studies indicates that children who attend nursery school make more rapid educational progress and display superior emotional adjustment in Infant School as compared with children who have had no preschool experience.[53] However, this research, while important, provides only limited insight into the processes by which the positive effects of nursery school are achieved. With the change in the magnitude and importance of early childhood schooling in Great Britain, it can be anticipated and hoped that future research efforts will be directed toward the systematic development and evaluation of varied preschool structures and alternative preschool curricula for the varied sample of children who participate in early educational programs.

CONCLUSION

This survey suggests that the present state of preschool education in England does not continue the leadership or reflect the innovative role that country once played in the early childhood education movement. From both current practice and research, it can be inferred that British early childhood schooling is dominated by outmoded philosophies and orientations, educationally as well as psychologically. There is little evidence to show that the preschool educational system has attended to and benefited from the recent theoretical and empirical contributions of behaviorism and of Piaget. This conclusion is reached whether one evaluates early childhood schooling from the vantage point of its program and facilities or from that of research and development.

From the Vantage Point of Program

The educational philosophies, theories, and models of Pestalozzi, Froebel, and McMillan and the psychoanalytic theory of Freud constitute the essential guiding principles of nursery programs as manifested in curricular practices and teacher behavior. The pervasive orientation of the nursery program is still the independent unfolding of the child's potential with accompanying emphasis on the social-emotional goals of development. Curriculum focus is on play and self-selection of materials. The integrity, freedom, and opportunity for growth of the young child are reflected in the respect, care, and freedom enjoyed by the children in nursery programs. Deliberate and planned articulation of cognitive goals and objectives is to a large extent absent. Cognitive stimulation and language development are not critical areas of concern.

From the Vantage Point of Facilities

An acute shortage of nursery school facilities exists in most parts of England. In general, fewer than 10 percent of children age 3 to 5 attend planned preschool programs. Further, most facilities devoted to preschool education do not provide for the child under the age of 3. The new Urban Programme will ameliorate, to some extent, this acute shortage by increasing the number of minority children receiving early schooling. However, attending a preschool, especially a state-supported nursery school, will remain a low-probability event for most children, if current allocations of support continue along their present course. At the present time, extra allocations are largely directed toward the critical expansion of secondary education and to compensatory programs for minority populations.

From the Vantage Point of Research and Development

The amount of ongoing and recent research in England related to early childhood schooling is both surprisingly meager and, with a few important exceptions, surprisingly disappointing. The studies encountered provide little novelty in the way of approach and procedure and many appear to be atheoretical, almost totally isolated from related research and contemporary theoretical developments in other countries. Further, almost no research or experimentation directly concerned with development and evaluation of curricula for the normal preschool child is being conducted. The few recent investigations dealing with this age group are primarily directed at compensatory education for minority and working-class children. Generally speaking, the special populations and accompanying cultural differences in language and customs of the diverse populations in England are not capitalized upon either in research or curriculum development.

Future Prospects

Given the limitations of the existing programs, the inadequate facilities, and the present lack of enthusiasm and experimentation, what then are the future prospects for early childhood schooling in England? In searching for an answer, one must appraise the strength of the professional group, the force of the scientific arm, the attitude and commitment of the government, and the current and future financial resources available for education.

The potential of the new Urban Programme is one critical factor. It represents the first major extension of government-sponsored nursery schooling since the war and could well serve as a catalyst for the early childhood schooling movement in England. First, despite its emphasis on the disadvantaged, it is under the jurisdiction of the Department of Education and Science rather than the Ministry of Health. This delegation of responsibility is in keeping with one of the major recommendations of the Plowden Report, i.e., that all programs for the child under 5 which include educational components come under the authority of the Department of Education and Science. This arrangement places nursery schooling in its proper educational context and reduces its traditional "social mission" flavor.

Second, and perhaps more important, is the emphasis of the Urban Programme on overcoming the *educational* handicaps of disadvantaged children. This consideration may make a significant impact on the instructional program. Curricula may have to be rethought and revised to be more consistent with this new emphasis. There will be a need for more systematic development of varied preschool structures and alternative preschool curricula for the varied sample of children in early childhood programs. In turn, the newly developed programs must be evaluated and appraised. Thus, there is a potential for narrowing the substantial gap which currently exists between British preschool practices and the implications of more generally contemporary theoretical and empirical research on early stimulation and cognitive development. Development of this potential is not dissimilar to the stimulation provided by Headstart and other programs in the United States which represented a dramatic expansion of interest and support by the national government and which resulted in increased cognizance of major issues in early childhood schooling.

A final note addresses itself to the talent and dedication of the individuals encountered in the course of making our observations. Individuals who were interviewed in government, in the universities, in nursery schools, and in parent groups were uniformly articulate, highly competent, and thoughtful. Perhaps most important are the devotion, interest, and love for children that this group shares. In other words, the talent and values are clearly available; what is lacking are financial and political catalysts and a thorough rethinking of the purpose, functions, and potential of early childhood schooling.

NOTES

1   M. McMillan, *The Nursery School,* Dent, London, 1927.
2   E. Howe, *Under Five: A Report on Nursery Education,* Conservative Political Centre, London, 1960; Willem Van der Eyken, *The Pre-*

school Years, Penguin Books, Aylesbury, England, 1969; *Children and Their Primary Schools* (Plowden Report), Report of the Central Advisory Council of Education, Her Majesty's Stationery Office, London, 1967, vols. I and II; and S. Yudkin, *O-5. A Report on the Care of Preschool Children,* National Society of Children's Nurseries, London, 1967.

3 Brian MacArthur, "Education Heading for Worst Years," *London Times,* Oct. 21, 1968, p. 1.

4 E. M. Dowley, "Early Childhood Education," in Robert L. Ebel (ed.), *Encyclopedia of Educational Research,* Macmillan, New York, 1969.

5 Laura A. Preston, "A London Venture: A Look at England's Schools," *Young Children,* vol. 22, 1966, p. 3.

6 J. L. Gewirtz, "Designing the Functional Environment of the Child to Facilitate Behavioral Development," and "The Role of Stimulation in Models for Child Development," in Laura L. Dittman (ed.), *Early Child Care,* Atherton Press, New York, 1968; Robert D. Hess and Roberta Meyer Bear (eds.), *Early Education: Current Theory, Research and Practice,* Aldine Publishing, New York, 1968.

7 W. H. L. Williams, Staff Researcher, National Foundation for Educational Research in England and Wales, personal communication, 1968.

8 N. Feshbach, M. Frances Klein, J. M. Novotney, and others, "|I|D|E|A| Guide to the Appraisal of Nursery Schools," Institute for Development of Educational Activities, Inc., Los Angeles, 1970.

9 McMillan, op. cit.

10 *The New Nursery School,* Nursery School Association of Great Britain and Northern Ireland, no. 72, London, 1962.

11 *Circular 8/60,* Department of Education and Science, London, 1960; *Addendum 65 to Circular 8/60,* December 1969 (Circular on Nursery Education).

12 F. J. Adams, E. L. M. Miller, M. Jeffreys, and W. Van der Eyken, *New Opportunities for Young Children,* Nursery School Association of Great Britain and Northern Ireland, London, 1968.

13 MacArthur, op. cit.

14 *Children and Their Primary Schools,* op. cit.

15 *Regulations and Syllabus for the Examination of the National Nursery Examination Board,* National Nursery Examination Board, London, 1970.

16 *Children and Their Primary Schools,* op. cit.

17 *Our Young Children,* Her Majesty's Stationery Office, London, 1969.

18 Susan Issacs, *The Educational Value of the Nursery School,* Nursery School Association of Great Britain and Northern Ireland, no. 45, London, 1954.

19 G. M. Goldsworthy, *Part-Time Nursery Education,* Nursery School Association of Great Britain and Northern Ireland, no. 75, London, 1964.

20 *Children and Their Primary Schools,* op. cit.

21 *Some Aspects of Piaget's Work,* 10th ed., National Froebel Foundation, London, 1968.

22 Van der Eyken, op. cit.

23 B. Keeley et al., *1,020 Playgroups—Survey 1968,* Pre-School Playgroups Association, London, 1968.

24 *The Supervisor's Handbook,* Pre-School Playgroups Association, London, 1967.

25 *Nursery and Playgroup Facilities for Young Children,* Nursery School Association of Great Britain and Northern Ireland, no. 76, London, 1967.

26 Keeley et al., op. cit.

27 Ibid.

28 Lady Allen Hurtwood, *Planning for Play,* Housing Centre Trust, London, 1968.

29 M. Ironside and S. Roberts, *Mathematics in the Primary School,* National Froebel Foundation, London, 1965; *Some Aspects of Piaget's Work,* op. cit.

30 J. Bowlby, "Maternal Care and Mental Health," World Health Organization Monograph no. 2, 1952.

31 M. L. Kellmer Pringle, *Deprivation and Education,* Longmans Green, London, 1965.

32 B. Bernstein, "Language and Social Class," *British Journal of Sociology,* 2, 1960, pp. 271–76; B. Bernstein, "Social Class and Linguistic Development: A Theory of Social Learning," in A. H. Halsey, J. Floud, and C. A. Anderson (eds.), *Education, Economy, and Society,* New York Free Press, New York, 1961; and B. Bernstein, "Social Class, Linguistic Codes, and Grammatical Elements," *Language and Speech,* vol. 5, 1962, pp. 221–40.

33 Dennis Lawton, *Social Class, Language and Education,* Routledge & Kegan Paul, London, 1968.

34 Williams, op. cit.

35 Ibid.

36 J. L. Frost and G. R. Hawkes, *The Disadvantaged Child, Issues and Innovations,* Houghton Mifflin, Boston, 1970.

37 Bernstein, op. cit.

38 B. Bernstein, Professor, Institute of Education, University of London, personal communication, 1968.

39 Ibid.

40 M. Donaldson and P. Wells, "The Development of Basic Cognitive Skills," paper presented at the Centre for Advanced Studies in the Developmental Sciences' Conference on Current Research in Great Britain on the Early Development of Behavior, University of Sussex, January 1969.

41 K. J. Connolly, "The Behavior of Preschool Children in a Group Context," paper presented at the Centre for Advanced Studies in the Developmental Sciences' Conference on Current Research in Great Britain on the Early Development of Behavior, University of Sussex, January 1969.

42 Pringle, op. cit.

43 J. K. Reynell, "The Construction of Normative Scales for the Assessment of Language Development," paper presented at the Centre for Advanced Studies in the Developmental Sciences' Conference on Current Research in Great Britain on the Early Development of Behavior, University of Sussex, January 1969.

44 J. Ryan, "Language Development in the Severely Subnormal," paper presented at the Centre for Advanced Studies in the Developmental Sciences' Conference on Current Research in Great Britain on the Early Development of Behavior, University of Sussex, January 1969.

45 P. J. Mittler, "Psycho-linguistic Skills in 4-year old Twins and Singletons," paper presented at the Centre for Advanced Studies in the Developmental Sciences' Conference on Current Research in Great Britain on the Early Development of Behavior, University of Sussex, January 1969.

46 P. E. Bryant, "Sensory Integration and the Perception of Orientation in Young Children," and "Age Changes in Learning Strategies," papers presented at the Centre for Advanced Studies in the Developmental Sciences' Conference on Current Research in Great Britain on the Early Development of Behavior, University of Sussex, January 1969.

47 J. H. W. Barrett, "A Neurophysiological Study of the Development of Information-processing in Short Term Memory Tasks in Normal and Slow Learning Children," paper presented at the Centre for Advanced Studies in the Developmental Sciences' Conference on Current Research in Great Britain on the Early Development of Behavior, University of Sussex, January 1969.

48 P. Woodward, "Non-cognitive Aspects of Problem Solving," paper presented at the Centre for Advanced Studies in the Developmental Sciences' Conference on Current Research in Great Britain on the Early Development of Behavior, University of Sussex, January 1969.

49 A. D. B. Clarke, "Factors Underlying the Use and Development of Equivalence Relations in Learning Transfer Situation," paper presented at the Centre for Advanced Studies in the Developmental

62 Early Schooling in England and Israel

Sciences' Conference on Current Research in Great Britain on the Early Development of Behavior, University of Sussex, January 1969.

50 J. and E. Newson, *Four Year Old in an Urban Community*, Allen and Unwin, London, 1968.

51 J. Newson and E. Newson, "A Longitudinal Study of Child Rearing Practices," "Situations of Conflict Between Mother and Child," and "The Development of Shape Perception in the Second Year of Life," papers presented at the Centre for Advanced Studies in the Developmental Sciences' Conference on Current Research in Great Britain on the Early Development of Behavior, University of Sussex, January 1969.

52 C. B. Hindley, "Longitudinal Research at Center for the Study of Human Development-Institute of Education, University of London," "Maternal Child Rearing Practices in Five European Cities," "Onset of Walking and its Relation to Other Factors," "Development of General Verbal Ability," and "A Factor Analytic Study of the Changing Nature of Early Abilities and of Their Relationships to Later Intelligence," papers presented at the Centre for Advanced Studies in the Developmental Sciences' Conference on Current Research in Great Britain on the Early Development of Behavior, University of Sussex, January 1969.

53 J. W. B. Douglas and J. M. Ross, "The Later Educational Progress and Emotional Adjustment of Children Who Went to Nursery School or Classes," *Educational Research*, vol. 7, 1966, p. 73; M. V. Harrold and M. H. Temple, "A Study of Children in the Admission Classes of Four Infant Schools, Making a Comparison Between Those Who Have Attended a Nursery School and Those Admitted Direct from Home," unpublished thesis, Child Development Centre, Institute of Education, University of London, 1959; and S. O'Sullivan, "A Comparative Study of Two Groups of Children in the Infant School: (1) Nursery Children, (2) Non-nursery Children," unpublished thesis, Child Development Centre, Institute of Education, University of London, 1958.

CHAPTER 3
EARLY SCHOOLING IN ISRAEL

Avima Lombard

ACKNOWLEDGMENTS

The author wishes to acknowledge the many individuals, and the organizations which they represent, who contributed to this study of early childhood schooling in Israel. Their cooperation and support as evidenced in the report which follows greatly deepened and expanded my own opportunity to understand and appreciate Israeli efforts in early childhood schooling from my vantage point at the Hebrew University of Jerusalem.

Although it is not possible to name all the individuals who contributed their talent and time, I would like to express my appreciation in particular to Nitza Naftali, National Supervisor of Preschool Education in Israel, for her active interest in and support of this effort to tell the story of early schooling in Israel. In addition, I would like to acknowledge Professor Abram Minkovitch, whose analysis of current preschool provision, of the pedagogical trends and ongoing research, and of future perspectives in early education, provided substantial background for the body of this report. Professor Moshe Smilansky of Tel Aviv University read the manuscript and offered valuable suggestions, many of which are included in the manuscript.

Finally, I would like to thank the observers who gathered much of the information on current preschool practices; the many preschool teachers who opened their classrooms for that purpose; and M. Frances Klein, for her assistance in the analysis of the classroom observations. The editorial assistance of Gretchen T. McCann is also gratefully acknowledged.

EARLY SCHOOLING IN ISRAEL

An examination of early childhood schooling in Israel first must be placed in the context of the unique and dramatic history of the country and of the peoples who compose it, for while Jews have lived in the land of Israel during all periods of history, its contemporary society is a society of immigrants.

The beginning of modern immigration dates from the latter part of the nineteenth century, when the nationalist movement of the "Lovers of Zion" stimulated the revitalization of the Hebrew language and the trek to Palestine of some 20,000 to 30,000 Eastern European Jews between 1882 and 1903. From that period to 1948, Palestine received four additional waves of Jewish immigrants, bringing the total number of Jews to approximately 650,000 on the eve of the proclamation of the state of Israel.

The period immediately following the establishment of the State was an era of unparalleled growth. Within 3 years, the Jewish population more than doubled, and by 1966, it had increased by more than 350 percent. Two-thirds of this increase was the result of immigration.

However, it was the nature of the immigrant population, as much as its magnitude, which has had the most significance for Israeli society, for, while 90 percent of the Jewish immigrants prior to the establishment of the state were European in origin, character, and outlook, more than half the immigrants after the proclamation were "Oriental."[1] These Jews came from the Islamic countries of the Middle East and Africa, and though there was great variation among them, for the most part they reflected the values and norms of the traditional cultures and pre-industrial economies of the countries from which they came. In contrast to their European counterparts, these immigrants were characterized by large and extended families, high birth rates, and low levels of literacy and vocational training.[2]

The size, speed, and nature of the immigration posed two serious possibilities for Israel: first, that the society would be pulled toward an Oriental rather than a Western culture (which its leadership considered it to be); second, that if the new immigrants were not quickly integrated, if they were not provided the means to equal opportunity, the society might polarize, with resultant ethnic conflict.[3]

Because education could reach the entire population of children, it became one obvious means by which the diverse population could become a unified society. The new country's commitment to education as a means of equalizing the opportunity of all its new citizens was exemplified in the Compulsory Education Law, enacted in September 1949, less than 8 months after the election of the first Israeli Parliament.[4] This law provided for 9 years of compulsory education for all children, including 1 year of kindergarten, beginning at age 5, and 8 years of primary school. Though unusual in a new nation, particularly a small and poor one with other, more urgent commitments, the inclusion of kindergarten as part of compulsory school attendance was a response to the needs of the substantial numbers of children whose parents neither spoke the Hebrew language nor were familiar with a modern educational system. At least 1 year of "preschool," it was felt, was a necessary prerequisite for later success in primary school. Indeed, many educators at the time argued for at least 2 years of kindergarten education, which had been the tradition within the Jewish community during the pre-state period.

In 1953, the Parliament passed a second law, the State Education Law, which provided for 2 major types of state-sponsored education: the general and the religious. In so doing, it eliminated the previous "trends" system, by which state-supported schools had been linked to various political parties and religious ideologies. Both types were united under a common aim based on ". . . the values of Jewish culture and the achievement of science, on love of the homeland and loyalty to the State and the Jewish people, on practice in agriculture and manual work, on 'halutzic' [pioneer] training, and on striving for a society built on freedom, equality, tolerance, mutual assistance, and love of mankind." Religious state education is distinguished from the general only in that its institutions are "religious as to their way of life, curriculum, teachers, and inspectors."[5]

The law also provided for state "recognition" of nonofficial independent schools. Under the law, such "recognized" schools are to be supervised by the Minister of Education and Culture, are to follow certain elements of the state curricula, and are entitled to financial assistance from the state. Primary among such "recognized" schools are those of the Agudat Israel, a political party representing the ultraorthodox Jews, as well as the schools of certain foreign Christian missionary societies.

Thus, within 5 years of its birth, Israel had provided for state-supported, compulsory early childhood schooling of both a general and religious nature.

STATE ADMINISTRATION AND SUPERVISION OF EARLY CHILDHOOD SCHOOLING PROGRAMS

Responsibility for early schooling lies with a special department within the Ministry of Education and Culture. A national supervisor serves as both director of the department and liaison between the department and other sections of the Ministry. Although the maintenance (and construction) of preschools is the responsibility of local authorities, the Ministry prescribes the curricula and program for all schools; provides for the certification, placement, and pay of all preschool teachers; and maintains a system of supervision over all preschool classes. Likewise, the Ministry of Education and Culture is directly responsible for the education of teachers for preschool programs and the teacher-preparation curricula.

In 1969, there were 36 field supervisors, working throughout 6 regions of the country. These supervisors, generally kindergarten teachers with at least 10 years of experience and additional training, are responsible for the supervision of 88 classes each. Because this large number makes on-site supervision difficult, a great deal of supervisory contact with teachers is maintained through group meetings and regional training sessions on curriculum topics deemed important by the Ministry. In addition, the supervisors are instrumental in the development of curricular guidelines and serve on a variety of committees within the Ministry dealing with problems of instruction. The national supervisor is responsible for the work and ongoing training of the field supervisors and makes field visits with each supervisor twice yearly, holds monthly meetings for all supervisory staff, and provides opportunities for improvement of each supervisor's knowledge and skills in a variety of settings.

Evolution of Government Policy

The orientation of government policy toward early childhood schooling (and toward education and social change in general) has gone through 3 discernible periods since the establishment of compulsory education.[6]

In the first period (the decade to 1957), there prevailed a commitment to "formal equality," the belief that, by giving equal opportunity and uniform treatment to all children, the vast differences within the immigrant populations would decrease. In addition, time, social pressures to disregard their cultural backgrounds, and certain emergency programs would provide the means by which the large numbers of Oriental Jews would adapt to the European-oriented pattern of the new country. Instead, the outcome was mass educational failure of the new immigrant children.[7] To give just one example, a 1957 survey of Hebrew and arithmetic achievement in grades 2 through 4 of a number of elementary schools in the Southern District revealed an overall failure rate of 50 percent among the children of Oriental parents, as compared with 12.5 percent among children of European origin.[8]

The evidence that equality of treatment did not yield equality in outcome led to the second phase (1957–1966), a growing recognition of the need for compensatory measures and a subsequent favoring, both administratively and materially, of the disadvantaged population. The actions taken during this phase for the most part reflected the belief that emergency and short-term administrative moves would produce the necessary results. The extent of the failure of such measures is suggested by the fact that in 1963 more than 85 percent of the dropouts from grades 6 and 7 in the elementary schools were children of "Oriental" parentage, almost double their proportion in the pupil population.[9] It must be noted, however, that the total dropout was relatively low.

The third phase (beginning in 1967) sought to overcome shortcomings of the first two. Given the widely divergent populations to be served, equality of educational opportunity could be achieved only by differential treatment according to their varying circumstances, abilities, and needs. In essence, this phase combined the goals of the first and second phases in a period of school reform during which the Ministry embarked upon a deliberate policy aimed especially at insuring the intellectual development and skill acquisition necessary to educational success and upward mobility of the educational disadvantaged population.[10]

Recognizing the importance of the first years of life to the child's intellectual development and subsequent school success, at the preschool level the new policy has resulted in the expansion of free kindergarten education to provide for increasing numbers of 3- and 4-year-old children from disadvantaged homes. In addition, in its curricula for the compulsory kindergarten year for 5-year-olds, the Ministry is promoting increased emphasis on intellectual development and readiness for formal instruction in the primary school. Finally, in recognition of the importance of the home to the child's total development, the Ministry is supporting programs of both research and action to determine how to bridge the cultural gap between the home and the school.

As will be evident in subsequent sections of this report, despite the significant change in the orientation of government policy, the current provision of early childhood schooling programs—the nature and content of preschool curricula and the orientation and practices of preschool teachers—now reflects all three phases. It is primarily in the research and development efforts related to the education of young children that the implications of the third phase are clearly exemplified.

PUBLIC PRESCHOOLS

In 1968–69, there were approximately 2,966 kindergartens in the Israeli public education system. This section of the report describes the population served by these kindergartens, the facilities and equipment available to most, the teachers and other support staff, and the basic orientation of the curricula. In addition, a description of classroom procedures during a typical kindergarten day is provided. The section concludes with a discussion of new programs and trends in the State provision of early childhood schooling.

The Population Served

In 1969, there were approximately 195,000 three- to five-year-old children in Israel, 22 percent of whom were Arabs or other minorities. As indicated above, the Ministry of Education must provide 1 year of free and compulsory kindergarten education, either general or religious, for all 5-year-olds. In 1969–70, there were approximately 60,790 five-year-olds in such state-sponsored classes. Further, in recognition of the special needs of a large number of young children, the Ministry is providing free preschool education for an increasing number of culturally and economically disadvantaged children at ages 3 and 4 (approximately 45,246 such children in 1969–70), with the goal of eventually providing programs for at least all 4-year-olds. It is estimated that approximately 70 percent of Jewish children aged 3 through 5 attend preschool classes. Only 25 percent of Arab children, the majority of whom live in villages, and other minority children of the same age range attend classes. However, most of these are 5-year-olds in the compulsory age group.[11]

Registration

Though registration is on a neighborhood basis, parents may choose either a general or a religious school. Usually there are enough classes of both types in a given locale to meet the needs of all families. However, since kindergarten for 5-year-olds is compulsory, preference is given to the admission of this age group, with the 3- and 4-year-olds assigned to the remaining available places. Class composition varies according to registration in a given year, though it generally reflects the ethnic representation of the local community. While an attempt is made to group the children by age, many classes have children ranging from 4 to 6 years.

Facilities

Classes for preschool children usually are housed in specially constructed preschool buildings. These buildings are located either near an elementary school, though quite separate from it, or in a central spot in local neighborhoods and villages. In the Arab sector, however, kindergartens are usually housed in the same building as the primary schools. The most common design for preschool buildings includes 2 classes in one building, with shared toilets, washroom, kitchen, and a kind of administration-reception area located near the front entry. Where preschools are housed in structures which were not designed for the purpose, however, single classes as well as 3 or 4 classes to a building sometimes are found.

Classrooms are generally well-equipped with a variety of materials. Adequate child-size furniture and major equipment are basic in all preschools. In addition, each teacher is provided with a budget for the purchase of educational supplies and materials so that, within a relatively short period of time, the physical aspects of the preschool classroom reflect the individual personality and interests of the teacher.

Some of the more commonly found facilities and materials are bulletin boards, child-size straight chairs, chalkboards, cubbies or lockers, phonograph and music-listening materials, running water, tables for working, toilets, balls, unit-table blocks, floor-crate blocks, library books, carriages and buggies, clay, collage materials, cooking materials (both toy and adult) and housekeeping toys, crayons, dolls and accessories, dress-up clothes and accessories, easels and accompanying materials, filmstrips, fingerpaints, hospital corner toys, math materials, mechanical toys, programmed materials, wood inlay puzzles, rhythm instruments, science materials, table toys, and both highly defined and creative play trucks, cars, trains, and boats.

Outdoor facilities and equipment receive less attention in Israeli public preschools. Although most outdoor play areas have adequate space and are properly fenced and cleared for safety purposes, the equipment is relatively sparse. This is especially true for playyards into which children from two classes stream at one time, bringing 70 children together with 3 to 4 swings, a few pieces of climbing apparatus, a sandbox, no tricycles, and few pieces of construction equipment. Woodworking tools are frequently provided where there are fewer children in the play area. A paucity of playground equipment was a condition noted also for English nursery schools (Chapter 2).

Kindergarten Teachers

In most cases, one certified teacher works with a class of 30 to 35 children. Preschool teachers are prepared in teacher-training colleges or seminaries where they take a 2-year program after at least 3 years of high school. There is an unfortunate tendency for the better students in teacher training institutes to move on to high school teaching and for the less successful ones to specialize as preschool teachers. However, the Ministry of Education and Culture maintains an ongoing program of in-service training and has made available an additional year of academic studies for those who qualify. In 1969, there were 3,988 kindergarten teachers employed throughout Israel. In the Jewish preschools, all teachers are women. But in the Arab schools, where men still retain the traditional role of educator and almost three-quarters of Arab elementary school teachers are male, a small number (5 percent) have carried this tradition to the kindergarten level.

Support Staff

Most teachers are assisted by an aide. Aides are women who are chosen for their willingness and ability to work with young children but who generally have had limited education and no formal training. In the standard division of tasks, the aide assumes responsibility for the housekeeping aspects of the nursery activities (preparation of snacks, clean-up after eating) and assists the teacher in routines such as dressing the children for outdoors, wash-up, etc. She is free to work directly with the children only between these tasks and rarely for more than half an hour at a time.

In addition, several specialists work with the preschools. A rhythmics teacher and a public health nurse visit regularly, and for children who need them, medical, dental, psychological, and other therapeutic services are available.

Curriculum

Traditionally, the orientation of the state-sponsored preschools has been to the all-round development of the child—physical, mental, linguistic, emotional, and social—with a considerable, though secondary, emphasis on school preparation. Since, in the beginning, the preschool setting was the framework within which children of immigrant parents were first exposed to the evolving rebirth of a common culture, the curriculum was primarily content-centered, with an emphasis on the acquisition of the Hebrew language and familiarity with the holidays, songs, and traditions of the Hebrew culture.

Although other more critical needs have been identified among the disadvantaged preschool population, many Israeli classes still reflect this emphasis. Their programs stress independent activity, self-expression through free play and creative activities, and personal orientation to the culture through celebrations and festivals, field trips, and songs. Within this general framework, however, there is a good deal of variability, depending on the school's religious orientation and the individual teacher's focus and interests.

Classroom Procedures

The preschool day begins at 8:00 A.M. and ends at 1:00 P.M.[12] There are no afternoon sessions and school is open 6 days a week. In Jewish schools, Saturdays are rest days; in Arab, the free day is Friday, these holidays corresponding in both instances to religious customs. Typically, the children arrive to find tables set up for quiet individual indoor activities. By 8:30, when all the children are assembled, chairs are moved into a circle, and half an hour of *ricuz* occurs during which the teacher raises a subject with the entire class and discussions and demonstrations follow. The subject is generally related to the overall theme or curricular area being dealt with at the time and frequently includes the teaching of songs and dances.

Since both nursery school and kindergarten classes have large numbers of children in them, most teaching is done in large groups, and relatively little attention is paid to the individual child's learning. Most teachers seem aware that individual children have specific needs, but they generally appear to lack the skills with which to seek out and work with an individual child. Moreover, many teachers seemingly consider such activity out of their realm. "Teaching" according to them involves large groups of children. The better the teacher, the larger the group she can handle or, more accurately, control. Conversely, small groups of children require less skilled teachers.

From the *ricuz* circle, the children move to semistructured indoor activities, generally related to the topic of the day. Tables are set up for creative work, but the children are free to choose a play corner, painting, or any other indoor activity. The children work and play in groups which are most often self-selected or minimally structured by the teacher. While the teacher directs classroom activities in a manner which is definitely controlling, at the same time she does allow for freedom and decision-making by the children.

Around 10:00 come clean-up and preparation for the mid-morning snack, which the aide has prepared for the whole class. After snack, most classes go outdoors for free play. The lack of outdoor equipment does not appear to affect the children's enjoyment of the outdoor period. An observer of outdoor playtime sees much activity in games, races, and creative play in all parts of the yard, with unusually few accidents, fights, or problems. This scene is common in spite of the fact that generally only one of the two staff members is in attendance and usually acts simply as a passive observer.

Between 11:30 and 12:00, the children are invited back into the classroom and assigned to tables where they work in small groups on a variety of semistructured formal learning tasks. The children's involvement in their tasks is striking. An atmosphere of self-controlled activity is characteristic of most Israeli classes. While the children do initiate contact with the teacher, there usually is a high degree of interaction among children, usually of a shared, cooperative, positive quality. When conflicts arise between children, they are generally treated gently. Teachers try to control the child's behavior verbally, through both reinforcement and reasoning. There is relatively little punishment in any form, and physical punishment is a rarity.

At 12:30, the circle of chairs is formed again and the children assemble as a class to listen to a story, sing songs, and summarize the day's activities. Dismissal is at 1:00.

A major variation in this daily routine occurs in preschools which have religious education as part of their curricular objectives. Approximately 23 percent of preschool classes fit this category, and their schedules include a short prayer period at the beginning of the day, blessings before and after eating, and a greater concentration on religious subjects throughout the curriculum. As a result, children in these classes have a little less time for each of the other activities.

Parents of preschool children are not actively included in this daily program of preschools of either type but are asked to help in preparation for holiday celebrations, in the decoration and maintenance of the preschool facility, and as extra hands on field trips. Preschool teachers report to the parents on the children's progress two or three times yearly. The report is in the form of a short scheduled conference at school during the evening hours. Many supervisors also have the preschool teachers make home visits at least once yearly. Additional compensation to teachers is provided for all such activity.

Most teachers keep very meager records on the children. The Ministry of Education requirements in this area are minimal and additional records are usually kept only in response to specific demands of the local supervisor.

New Developments

As the preceding description reveals, the regimen of the typical Israeli kindergarten classroom relies heavily on the child's initiative and autonomy and on prior social and intellectual stimulation in the home.

However, as previous sections suggest, by the late 1950s it had become painfully evident that the traditional approach was not suited to the large numbers of Israeli children from disadvantaged and immigrant homes, especially those of "Oriental" background. This realization stimulated a search for new programs to meet the needs of these children and to close the "cultural gap" between them and their more advantaged peers. Though this search continues (and will be discussed in some detail in the section on research), two new programs have been developed and are being used with substantial numbers of disadvantaged preschool children—the Intensive Instruction program and the Directive Instruction program.

Intensive Instruction Approach   The Intensive Instruction program[13] is currently recommended by the Ministry of Education and Culture as one approach for classes with a high proportion of disadvantaged preschool children. In this program, teachers are asked to evaluate the children in terms of the deficits with which they come to the preschool class and to assess their progress in terms of processes as well as products. Individual and small group work is encouraged rather than the teaching of large groups. Emphasis is placed on language and perceptual skills, fundamental concepts in mathematics and science, persistence in dealing with problematic didactic materials, and an increased awareness of the immediate environment. Parent involvement, stronger emotional ties between teacher and child, increased reinforcement for classroom activity, concentrated attention on the child's performance, and increased verbalization are suggested means for meeting the problem of the disadvantaged child's negative self-image and his comparative lack of readiness for any school situation.

In her description of the fundamentals of the Intensive Instruction program, Naftali suggests that this preschool program is built upon two axes. The one is the child's free play and creativity; the other is the supportive, directing teacher who looks for opportunities to move the child along on a steady course of development. The balance struck between these two is the product of interaction between each teacher and her class.

Directive Instruction Approach   Dr. Sarah Smilansky, who has been active in research relating to young disadvantaged children in Israel for over 15 years, has developed an alternate approach to the education of these children. Her view is that disadvantaged preschoolers require a relatively structured environment, with more direction and guidance than is currently accepted in preschools.

The Directive Instruction approach proposed by Smilansky deals in the same content areas as the Intensive Instruction program but differs in emphases and in teaching methods proposed. Its basic premise is that disadvantaged children require teaching techniques and a learning environment which are different from those of the regular kindergarten. The special environment should be aimed at advancing children in those areas which are directly related to school success—cognitive language and efficient learning habits. Smilansky suggests that increasing knowledge and experience is less important than using that with which the child is familiar as a basis for the organization and deepening of his knowledge.

Language skills are important but should aim at increased expressiveness rather than mere talkativeness. In addition, the child must be helped to acquire perseverance and concentration in tasks, the ability to plan ahead, and the ability to be critical. Existing norms cannot be used as criteria for success with disadvantaged children. The enrichment program, therefore, should be paced to each individual's growth pattern and rate insofar as possible.

The daily program is fully scheduled. The child is in kindergarten 5 hours daily, and during this period it is more difficult for him to move from periods of concentration to free activity and then back to concentrated work than to maintain a level of discipline throughout the day. The directive teacher of disadvantaged preschoolers must be more actively involved in all aspects of the day's work than must a regular kindergarten teacher since she must miss no opportunity for cognitive language development and also she cannot rely on the children to learn from their environment without regular and directed guidance. Such directed, defined intervention is necessary for all forms of art activity as well as for cognitively oriented tasks. According to Smilansky, the child needs to learn fundamental techniques before he can express himself freely in painting, movement, dramatics, etc.

In general, the atmosphere in a Directive Instruction classroom is one of humming activity, with a teacher who seems to be everywhere at once. There is, however, a notable absence of spontaneity among the children, and free movement from activity to activity is discouraged.

Combined Kindergarten/Primary   Another recent innovation is the move by the Ministry of Education and Culture to establish kindergartens combined with the first and second grades of the primary schools. In these institutions, which are somewhat similar to the British Infant Schools, instruction in the rudiments of the 3 R's begins at age 6, but the general atmosphere and regimen are more like those of the typical kindergarten than of the typical elementary school—with emphasis on individual and group work, self-expression and creative play, direct experience, and the manipulation of concrete and didactic materials. However, because of the special and separate nature of the preschool, there is a good deal of resistance on the part of preschool personnel to this proposal (as there has been to both the Intensive Instruction and the Directive Instruction programs). Nonetheless, initial experiments with the new structure have been particularly successful with children of new immigrants and those from culturally disadvantaged homes, and several additional experimental mergers are planned for the next few years.

OTHER PROGRAMS FOR THE YOUNG CHILD

There exist a number of additional organizations seeking to meet the educational needs of the young child. Primary among them are the kibbutzim (or collective settlements), a variety of volunteer women's organizations, and the Ministries of Labor and Health.

The Kibbutzim

Though their current membership includes only 4 percent of the total school-age population in Israel, the kibbutzim represent a distinctive aspect of early childhood education in Israel.

The history of the kibbutz is intimately linked with the Zionist movement at the turn of the century and the early waves of Jewish immigrants who returned to Palestine during that period. The first kibbutz was established in 1909 in Degania, its founders dedicated to the ideal of building a new society based on communal labor, the total equality of its members, and a return to the soil for sustenance and survival.[14] In this new organization, the economic, social, cultural, and psychological welfare of all members was the responsibility of the collective group. Indeed, *kibbutz* is the Hebrew word for "group."[15]

All activities previously associated with the family unit were to be taken over by the group. The communal dining hall became the symbol and the center of collective life, serving not only as the locus for meals and social events but also for communal government, in which each member had an equal voice. Succeeding waves of immigrants followed the example of the pioneers in Degania, and by 1945, there were 116 kibbutzim in Palestine. Today there are an estimated 230 kibbutzim in Israel, their populations ranging from 150 to 1,500 and, occasionally, even more.

In the kibbutzim, education is an integral part of child rearing. Schooling, in the sense of parents entrusting their children to an institution, begins at birth and continues until age 18.[16] Infants usually are placed in the kibbutz "baby home" when they are 4 days old, and they live and are raised with their peers until they reach maturity, spending a portion of each day with their parents. Primary responsibility for the care of the infant and, later, the child is entrusted to "metaplot," women of the kibbutz who are especially trained for that function.

The practice of communal child rearing and early "socialization" in the kibbutzim rests on several bases—ideological, practical, and psychological.[17] In line with the commitment to total equality, women were to be "freed" from the daily demands of child rearing so that they might take an equal part in the work of the new settlements. To insure that the settlements would survive beyond one generation, children were, from the beginning, to be accustomed to collective life, to be raised as "kibbutz type of people" who would carry on the traditions of kibbutz life. At a time when the remainder of the settlement had to sleep in tents or wooden huts, decent housing for the children, at least, could be provided through a single dwelling. And the "bourgeois" past, with the home as the center of both selfish interest and psychological strain between generations, could be overcome by the provision of trained "professional" child rearers.

Though practices vary from kibbutz to kibbutz, most children live in a baby home and then a toddlers' home until they are of nursery school age. At that time, usually between 3 and 4 years, the child joins the kindergarten house where he lives and is taught with a group of 18 to 27 other children whose ages may range from 3 to 7 years. Education of the nursery children is the responsibility of a kindergarten teacher, who, along with the metapelet, is also responsible for their feeding and care.[18] Education is viewed as an all-embracing process whose aim is to develop the whole child, and design of the children's house supports the integration of living and learning; the classroom facilities are usually included within the living structure and thus the functions of daily life—playing, eating, sleeping, and doing classwork —all occur in the same place.[19] The parents, who live in houses or apartments today, always are close by.

During the 8-hour "school" day, activities might include a lesson in shared responsibility through cleaning the rooms as well as more typical kindergarten subjects. Lessons in the 3 R's for the 6-year-olds are included within the kindergarten regime. Thus, what is usually thought of as the first grade of primary school is typically bypassed, and children in the 7-year age group enter the second grade directly upon leaving the nursery group.

Common to most kibbutzim is the progress of the child through the early steps of his education on the basis of "readiness" rather than on class structuring and sequencing. The early years of school are essentially nongraded. The kibbutzim maintain close contact with a central psychological guidance center and are generally prepared to experiment with and try new techniques and materials to produce what they consider to be better educational results.

Though considered to be part of the state education system, the kibbutzim maintain a greater degree of authority over their schools than do other state schools.[20] They exercise considerable influence over the assignment of teachers to the kibbutzim and operate special teacher-training seminaries which have the formal status of state institutions. In addition, they provide in-service training for their teachers and determine, to large degree, their own curricula.

Recent developments in the kibbutzim suggest that the tradition of communal child rearing may alter significantly in the years to come.[21] Increasing affluence, as evidenced through the availability of more material goods (including radios and televisions), especially among the more established kibbutzim, and the addition of industrial work to be performed by kibbutz settlements, is changing the original orientation to the land and to the simple life. However, more significantly, the younger generation of kibbutzim Sabras, those born and bred in Israel, is arguing for greater participation of the family in the raising of children. Many kibbutzim now allow the children to sleep in their parents' rooms, and some have abolished the children's houses altogether.

Volunteer Programs

A variety of volunteer movements maintain preschool day care centers, attended by approximately 9,000 two- to four-year-old children. Some 2 dozen religious, political, and civic organizations provide such day care, but the bulk of the centers (135 with 7,500 children) are maintained by 2 large women's organizations—WIZO (Women's International Zionist Organization) and Irgun Imahot Ovdot (Working Mother's Organization). These programs provide children of working mothers with care from about 6 months to school age. The content of the daily program varies from center to center, but in general, it is of a custodial rather than an educational nature until about age four.

Ministry of Labor

Day care services of a somewhat different nature have recently been set up by the Ministry of Labor in conjunction with local authorities. Extended-day kindergartens in industrial centers are provided for kindergarten children whose mothers work and for whom there is no other day care available. In the extended-day kindergartens, children receive lunch, rest, and are involved in activities supervised by a qualified kindergarten teacher. These facilities adjust their daily time schedules to provide the coverage essential to the work schedules of the mothers.

Ministry of Health

For the very young, the Ministry of Health maintains a highly developed program of "Mother and Child Centers" for the pre- and postnatal care of infants. An extremely large percentage of Israeli mothers take advantage of this program, since the care given is free of charge and the centers have earned a reputation for excellence over the years. Emphasis in the program is on health, nutrition, and physical care. A mother and her child are seen regularly until the child is 3 or 4 years old. Health records are kept on the children, and courses on the basic elements of child health and care are available for the mothers. The public health nurse with whom the mother has regular contact also acts as general consultant and child-care guide.

RESEARCH

As indicated above, it is in the research and development efforts of Israeli investigators that the impact of the third phase of government policy with respect to the education of young children is most clearly evidenced. To a significant degree, the limited resources available for the support of research are directed toward the acquisition of knowledge and the identification of programs which will be more effective in meeting the educational needs of disadvantaged children and in closing the gap between them and their more advantaged peers.

Current research in early childhood education can be described under 3 general categories: (1) research directed at the manipulation of classroom variables, such as curriculum, methods of instruction, and class composition; (2) research which focuses on the educational environment of the home and the involvement of parents in the education of their children; and (3) research directed toward methods for assessing the behavior of young children.

Manipulation of Classroom Variables

Intensive Instruction vs. Directive Instruction (Smilansky)   The Ministry of Education, together with the Henrietta Szold Institute for Research in the Behavioral Sciences, has been involved in large-scale longitudinal study in which the effectiveness of the Intensive Instruction approach was being compared with that of the Directive Instruction approach.[22] Smilansky, who spent several years examining special programs for the intellectual advancement of preschool children, proposed that reading skills can be most effectively taught in the kindergarten (with children aged 5); that teaching such skills would be especially helpful for disadvantaged children as they progressed into the lower school grades; and that a Directive Instruction environment is best suited for the acquisition of early reading skills.

This study, which included approximately two thousand children, two-thirds of whom were in poverty areas, was conducted through 1971. The major variables examined were

1   Age of commencement of instruction—kindergarten vs. first grade.
2   Method of reading instruction—phonetic vs. global.
3   Curricular framework—intensive vs. directive.

The first phase of the study began in 1967. The kindergarten classes in this phase were assigned to either the Directive Instruction approach or the Intensive Instruction approach. Within each framework, the classes were subdivided for reading instruction using either global or phonetic reading systems. Results of the first year's work showed marked differences in achievement between the advantaged and the disadvantaged children. The greatest overall achievement was in classes with the Directive Instruction framework (p>.05). The global reading instruction was generally more effective than the phonetic system.

In 1968, the program was repeated with staff who were more experienced and familiar with the new curriculum and schedule demands. A second group of kindergarten children was selected and divided into 2 reading instruction treatments. The curricular framework was no longer under study, and only the Directive Instruction program was used. Results of this year's work were similar to those of the previous year. Primarily, it was found that teaching reading in the kindergarten was both feasible and in no way detrimental to an atmosphere of freedom and creativity. Children from privileged backgrounds benefited most from reading instruction, while, in the disadvantaged group, a marked relationship appeared between intelligence and achievement. There was little difference in results for the 2 methods of reading instruction, though the global method was generally more successful for poor readers. The relatively low level of success in assimilating reading techniques and in comprehension among disadvantaged children raised the question as to whether exposure to reading instruction was a total waste or whether a form of latent learning had occurred which would be reflected in achievement in later years.

In the third year of the study, first-grade teachers were taught to use the different instructional techniques, and the children were divided into 4 groups: children who had had previous reading instruction (experimental groups) continued in their 2 instructional treatment groups as in kindergarten (phonetic or global instruction); entering first-graders (control groups) were divided into global or phonetic instruction groups. There was an equal number of advantaged and disadvantaged children in each of the four groups.

Findings at the end of grade one were somewhat different from those of previous years. There were still significant, though smaller, differences between the advantaged and the disadvantaged children's total reading achievement. There was no difference between the experimental and control groups among the advantaged children, and although there were also no differences between the 2 groups of disadvantaged children in reading skills (15 percent of both groups remained nonreaders), the children who began reading in kindergarten were significantly better in reading comprehension than those who began reading in first grade. Additionally, a record of "failure" in kindergarten appeared to have no effect on later learning.

As to the educational environment, it was reported that by the end of the first grade there were no differences between children who were in the Directive and Intensive Instruction groups in kindergarten.

Although final results will not be in until this group of children has completed second grade, the Ministry of Education has tentatively rejected the idea of using the Directive approach in preschool but is seriously considering the introduction of a limited reading program in selected kindergartens.

Readiness Skills (Lipschitz)   Government plans for reading instruction will probably take into account the results of another recent study, by Lipschitz, in which early reading instruction was preceded by a concentrated program in readiness skills.[23] This study focused on language skills, concept development, and perceptual discrimination. Halfway through the year, reading instruction was introduced in small groups, starting with those children who were most advanced in the readiness skills. The children were given both readiness and reading tests at the end of the kindergarten year, and results indicated that instruction produced significant achievement for all children when compared with uninstructed controls. As in the Smilansky study, the advantaged children learned to read in a short time, and the disadvantaged children did not. It was suggested, however, that the readiness skills acquired by the disadvantaged children would enhance their learning to read in first grade. The specific program for reading instruction probably will undergo several changes in the course of the next few years, but it does appear that reading studies will have an impact on the total kindergarten curriculum.

Science and Mathematics (Chen)   Work in science and mathematics with somewhat similar goals is underway. The Elementary School Science Project established at Tel Aviv University under the direction of a biophysicist, Dr. David Chen, introduces kindergarten (as well as older) children to concepts and processes basic to both science and mathematics. It depends heavily on materials which the children manipulate and discuss together in small groups. Because the project requires small group rather than total class "frontal" teaching, to which most Israeli teachers are accustomed, an in-service teacher education component is required. The cooperation of the Instructional Television Center (see below) has been enlisted for this purpose, and a film contrasting the two teaching modes has now been prepared.

One of the interesting features of Chen's work is his effort to deal with problems of implementing, not merely developing, a new curriculum. The same attention that has gone into building upon principles of child development and learning in developing curriculum materials has been devoted, also, to developing change strategies with the schools. Although this approach results in a relatively complex process, the chances of losing the new methodology and introducing only new content has been vastly reduced. It may be more difficult to "sell" this approach to funding agencies but, undoubtedly, the results will be superior to conventional curriculum projects which usually do little more than produce new materials.

Socio-Dramatic Play (Smilansky) Smilansky's research has brought to light a variety of areas in which the kindergarten curriculum might be changed. Observation of socio-dramatic play among preschool children indicated differences in play patterns between culturally advantaged and disadvantaged children.[24] The latter appear to be less flexible; they do not role-play or use imagination in a dramatic play situation. Instead, they copy known patterns of behavior, such as those of their parents. Cooperative play is minimal in their socio-dramatic play and toys are used functionally rather than imaginatively. Speech connected with the dramatic play situation tends to revolve around the manipulation of players rather than the dramatization of the situation.

It was suggested that differences in patterns of socio-dramatic play reflected differences in cognitive ability between the 2 groups of children. Lack of sustained thought, rapid movement from one activity to another, constriction by visual stimuli, and limited language are commonly found behaviors in disadvantaged children. Culturally advantaged children do not generally manifest these deficiencies, which may be due to their ability to recognize and to integrate factors in their immediate environment into usable conceptual frameworks. Changing socio-dramatic play patterns in disadvantaged children, therefore, was suggested as a possible means of promoting such integrative and cognitive ability.

Socio-dramatic play skills were promoted by the teachers in 3 selected groups of preschool children. Over a period of 3 weeks, in 1½-hour daily sessions, the teachers worked to provide the children with direct guidance in play techniques and to sharpen and enrich impressions from their immediate environment. Comparison of these classes with 2 uninstructed control classes showed that the experimental children gained in participation in socio-dramatic play, in speech output, and in language structure and content. There was also a rise in the level of dramatic play, in ability to assume roles, and in sustained interest in the dramatic play situation.

No major changes have occurred in the preschool curriculum as a result of this study, though it has drawn attention to socio-dramatic play as yet another area in which children can be described as culturally disadvantaged and in which teacher intervention apparently can be helpful.

Learning Conditions (Smilansky)   The effects of different learning conditions on young children's success with tasks related to reading and arithmetic skills were the subject of a further study by Smilansky.[25] Approximately two hundred children aged 4 to 6, drawn from educationally disadvantaged backgrounds, were divided into 5 matched experimental instruction groups. Their preschool teachers were given guidance in the use of one of five experimental teaching conditions, as follows:

1   General instruction only—the traditional kindergarten approach, but with a smaller group of children than in the regular class setting.
2   Active guidance in finding the basic principle for the specific activity.
3   Guidance in performance and a clear frame of reference—the teacher did not help find principles but set the stage for learning.
4   Setting specific achievement goals for each child according to his ability—the teachers move each child forward at his individual pace.
5   Verbal control of tasks—the teacher worked toward control of impulsivity, a critical attitude, analysis of errors, and verbal description of activity.

The criterion tasks given to all children following 8 to 12 instructional sessions consisted of matching letters, words, and a picture in given test situations. Results indicated that the traditional instruction situation is helpful only for 5-year-old children with a measured IQ over 90. In the other instruction treatments, however, gains were significant, with few differences either within or between the groups.

Smilansky concluded that it is false to assume that disadvantaged children can act on a teacher's instructions as is usually demanded of them in the preschool setting. They need active help in finding the underlying principles of a task and direct guidance in learning rules for discovery and learning. She suggests that learning is intensified for these children when they are guided by means of verbal control of their behavior. Findings from this study were used in setting the guidelines for the Directive Instruction system.

Body Movement (Bilsky-Cohen) A somewhat different curricular study has been conducted by researchers at the Hebrew University of Jerusalem. Bilsky-Cohen, in collaboration with Melnick, has developed and experimented with techniques for fostering concept-learning through body movement.[26] Her early work with second-grade children yielded promising results, and during the 1969–70 academic year the program was experimentally adapted for use with kindergarten children.

The experiment involved 3 kindergarten classes, 2 of which were considered socially disadvantaged. The third class, in a different neighborhood, was composed of middle-class children and was selected for comparison purposes. A battery of pretests was administered to all the children. The classes in the disadvantaged area were then divided on a matched-sample basis according to age, sex, and pretest measures. One-half of the children in each of these classes were assigned to the experimental program while the other half were considered matched controls.

The instructional program involved 3 weekly lessons lasting 30 minutes each. Primary concepts taught were those of form, space, size, quantity, time, and basic movements. In addition, it was hoped that the children's level of ability would improve in the following areas: observation and differentive concentration, familiarity with their own body, shifting, spatial orientation, coordination, and verbal description of movements. During the instructional period, the control groups were engaged in organized games and similar physical activity. There was no special program for the comparison group of middle-class children.

The major variable to be examined was the effectiveness of using structured movement lessons in teaching concepts. This involved comparison of children in the experimental groups with their matched counterparts in the same class. Approximately ten post-tests were used as measures of intelligence, rigidity, body awareness, school-readiness, size, form, spatial orientation, direction, and conversation.

Specific results of the experiment cannot yet be presented. However, the investigators have reported several findings relating to the children's behavior and learning patterns. All the children were at least 5 years old, yet their knowledge of the parts of their bodies, descriptive adjectives, and logical thinking was minimal. The concept of "cause and effect" appeared to be almost nonexistent. The level of concentration was very low and the span of attention short. The children seemed to have a distinct lack of self-control and all outside stimuli distracted them. This was especially marked in free-movement, when large motions, speed and strength, free use of the whole room, and self-organization into groups were required. Such activity is not usually demanded of the children in the kindergarten setting and they apparently found the self-control involved very difficult.

All these handicaps were more pronounced with kindergarten children than had been observed with the second-grade children with whom the investigators had previously worked. An additional area of difficulty was encountered in the low level of cooperation between the children even when the task called for it. Much of the program requires such cooperation, and as a result, instruction was slower than anticipated.

In general, there appeared to be progress in all areas, with definite increase in levels of accurate observation, verbal discrimination, and differentiation between relatively fine shades of variation in the concepts taught. The children learned to relate verbal labels to relevant actions or situations, and their span of concentration and speed of reaction increased considerably.

Montessori Evaluation Several years ago, the Ministry of Education and Culture introduced the Montessori system into a few selected preschool classes. In line with their policy of exploring new techniques and keeping up, insofar as possible, with new developments in preschool education, the supervisors of preschool education were eager to evaluate the effectiveness of a modified Montessori system in the local schools. Following 2 years of generally positive subjective evaluation of the experimental programs by the supervisors, the Ministry of

Education and Culture examined the effectiveness of the system in terms of testable results in the children. All children were given a local adaptation of the Caldwell Preschool Inventory. At the end of the school year, the same test was administered as a post-test.

Results indicated that although there was little gain in language skills, children in the Montessori-style classes made significant progress in perceptual discrimination skills and in their approach to problem-solving situations. Eighteen classes were equipped with the special Montessori materials, and it was decided to continue with their use. For kindergarten-age disadvantaged children, they appear to constitute a helpful educational framework. No effort is being made, however, to expand it to other similar preschools.

Educational Television   Television is relatively limited in Israel but receives quite devoted attention. A single channel provides 4 hours of viewing each evening, without advertising, as a public service similar to that provided by the BBC in England. But the Instructional Television Center in Tel Aviv, a department of the Ministry of Education and Culture, operates throughout the day with a full-time staff of experienced educators and television specialists. Reference was made above to the use of film in teacher education.

Two phases of a study of the effectiveness of incorporating television instruction in the preschool curriculum have now been completed.

In the first phase, approximately 25 fifteen-minute programs were shown to about 30 preschool classes. The films dealt with mathematics and science concepts, children's stories, and situations requiring the awareness and identification of familiar emotions. Programs were first evaluated with 2 to 4 classes in which there was no specific preparation for the day's subject. This yielded a measure of the effectiveness of each program in teaching specific content. Another 27 classes were shown the telecasts at a later date. Teachers of these classes previewed each program at the television studio, at which time they were given a teaching guide and worksheets for the children relating to the subject matter of the program. The actual telecast was thus only one element in the total instructional sequence for each subject. Evaluation was based on teachers' reports, questionnaires, and observation by the preschool supervisor.

The results of the first year indicated that when television was used as the only element in instruction, the children's learning was poor.[27] Those telecasts integrated in a total instructional sequence produced good results, however, as reported by the teachers.

In the second year, it was decided to evaluate only telecasts integrated within a total instructional sequence. The program was tested in 12 kindergartens which enrolled both advantaged and disadvantaged children from 3 through 5 years of age. Each group within the experimental classes was matched with a control group in which the same instructional materials were taught, but without the telecasts. The specific questions posed for the second-year evaluation were

1 Is television an appropriate medium for preschool education and what should be its contribution?
2 Should the telecasts be of an instructional nature or should they be limited to enrichment? Should the subject matter arise from school or life outside school?
3 How will children of this age react to television, both in school and in general? Should they be in some way active during the telecasts?
4 What should the rate of telecasts be? What percentage should be allocated to general basic concepts, to science, to social studies, etc.?
5 What will be the reaction of the teachers? How can parents become involved?

The results of the second-year evaluation indicated that the television component contributed little to the educational achievement of the lower-age group of the educationally disadvantaged children. As a result, the television series is currently being revised. Guiding this work are a number of additional questions which derive from the evaluation and from the field experience:

1 Through what medium should the televised material be presented: a teacher or other personality, children, puppets, animation, etc.?
2 Are approaches such as realism and imagination, conflict as a source of motivation, and self-discovery appropriate at this age?
3 Should the telecasts be independent of each other or a series? Should the same concept be presented through several approaches?
4 Should additional programs be produced for the children to watch at home?
5 Is there any way to differentiate subjects for different ages and levels?

Integration as a Variable (Feitelson) The question of the effects of integration on behavior and achievement in preschool classes has been studied by Feitelson of the Hebrew University of Jerusalem.[28] Feitelson set out 7 objectives for this study:

1 To determine whether integrating lower-income, culturally disadvantaged and upper-middle-class children at an early age stimulates the intellectual functioning and social development of the disadvantaged group.

2 To compare the 2 groups in close proximity and under identical conditions pertaining to socioeducational opportunities, in order to identify and expose components of deficits revealed by the disadvantaged children which result in an intellectual gap and social distances as well as strangeness between the groups.

3 To use insights and knowledge gained with regard to the differences between the groups in order to define and provide for appropriate social and educational opportunities, aimed at ameliorating and treating the specific needs which will be pointed up by this constant comparison.

4 To observe whether such opportunities developed by the project can be successfully applied to a homogeneous group of lower-income, culturally disadvantaged children.

5 To study the attitudinal and behavioral reactions both at school and at home of both groups of children and their families to the social interaction with each other.

6 To study whether cultural deprivation is a cumulative process (so that despite integration and equal socioeducational opportunities in the school setting, the gap between the 2 groups of children will grow wider from year to year), or whether the differences will tend to diminish as a result of the project framework.

7 To serve as a demonstration and in-service training center for personnel of various disciplines—more specifically, to enhance the sensitivity to socioeducational problems of preschool children and develop skills to cope with them effectively.

Ninety-six 3-year-old children in 4 experimental preschool classes were selected for this program which was underway for 3 years. One-third of the children in each of 3 of the selected classes were disadvantaged and these classes were considered heterogeneous. The fourth class had a homogeneous population, where all the children were disadvantaged.

Three additional homogeneous classes, two with disadvantaged children and one with middle-class children, were selected as control classes for the purposes of study. Children in all 7 classes (N = 168) were pretested at the beginning of the 3-year period.

An intensive effort was made to bring the teachers in the experimental classes to a point of readiness and ability to work with individual children and to release them from the traditional curriculum centering on Hebrew culture and holidays. Close records were kept on the children and their families, and this information, in addition to individual testing, observation, interviews with parents and teachers, is being used in evaluating the success of the experimental treatments.

Post-testing was completed in May 1970, and, although complete data are not yet available, preliminary findings indicate that heterogeneous groups gained significantly on all but one test, a nonverbal intelligence measure. Feitelson views these results hesitantly, however, since it is possible that an initial selection factor may have been at work with only interested, upward-bound parents having sent their children to the special mixed classes.

Two interesting analyses are based on classroom observation. Play activity was systematically mapped so as to assess play interests and friendship patterns. It was found that the main variable in emphasis on one play form as against another was the class teacher. Play patterns changed as teachers changed and for each teacher's classroom play patterns persisted even when the children changed. No difference in choice of play corner was found between culturally disadvantaged and advantaged children, with sex of the child acting as the significant factor in play choice.

A second type of classroom observation involved recording social contacts made by a child in a given 1-hour period. Categories of Social Contact Units (SCU) were identified as cooperation, contact, vicinity, looking at or listening to, ignoring, rejection, and aggression. The SCU records kept on a child indicated interaction with advantaged or disadvantaged children, and by whom contact was initiated. Preliminary findings from these observations indicate that by the second year there was little difference in the amount of interaction for the 2 groups of children. Advantaged children mixed predominantly with their own group, as did the disadvantaged children, but the latter also interacted more with adults. This may be due to adult initiation of contact as part of guidance and intervention techniques.

In many cases, there were children active in the same play corner with no interaction whatsoever, and it was found that interaction in itself does not necessarily develop into mutual play. Feitelson suggests that for indoor play activities, especially, life experiences are influential. Where it was possible to equalize the experiences of the 2 groups, by a trip to the airport for instance, the play contact for all children dealt with airports, whereas this had previously been the exclusive domain of the advantaged.

Final analyses of the data will yield more exact findings, but this study has been watched closely by educators in Israel for indications of guidelines by which to determine the degree to which classroom composition may be affecting children's performance. Emotional overtones are clearly evoked here, since local educators would like to have proof that integration produces better-educated children.

Classes in the Feitelson study were unusually small and the teachers were closely supervised and guided. As these conditions were not typical of Israeli preschools, the Feitelson programs cannot be viewed as models for integrated classes. An attempt to create such a model is currently underway, however, under the sponsorship of the Ministry of Education.

Nachlaot Project (Naftali)   The Nachlaot project in Jerusalem is under the direct supervision of Mrs. Naftali, national supervisor of preschool education. Schools in the Nachlaot area draw children from both an established middle-class neighborhood and an old, crowded near-slum. In this project, children are assigned to classes in such a way as to insure a balance between the educationally advantaged and disadvantaged. Because of the differences in ability levels, integrated classes were previously avoided, and thus the Nachlaot project is focusing on educational techniques for handling such groupings.

Twelve kindergartens and 12 first grades in 5 schools have been assigned an extra teacher, who works 2 hours daily in each class. Classes have been arranged so as to provide interest corners and to allow for work in small groups. Teaching is primarily in small groups with children organized heterogeneously for general activity learning, homogeneously for special work with the tutoring teacher, or in self-selected units around interest corners. The curriculum focuses on basic skills and teachers are encouraged to innovate and experiment.

Nachlaot Project Evaluation   The Nachlaot project was undertaken without specific plans for evaluation, and so there are no experimental controls. A group from the Hebrew University Department of Psychology has become interested in evaluating the project, however, and has taken initial steps to devise questionnaires and rating sheets to be used in an evaluative study.[29]

In addition to appraising the effectiveness of the Nachlaot project, the study proposes to examine whether the heterogeneous groupings will effect new patterns of relations between the children. Only the kindergartens will be studied and evaluation will be based on observation of interaction-sociometric choices of the children; the teachers' rating of each child on measures of dominance, sharing, dependence, and independence; and the children's attitudes by asking them to respond to pictures of children who are clearly either "Western" or "Near-Eastern" in appearance.

Home and Parent Involvement

Parent Involvement (Smilansky)　In the course of her work on the development of new programs for the education of disadvantaged preschool children, Smilansky explored the possibility of drawing parents into a closer working relationship with the schools.[30] Visits to homes of preschool children in her studies indicated that lower-class parents approve of and want to cooperate with the school but do not know how to do so.

Later, a pilot study was begun by Smilansky to investigate methods by which parents could be more actively included in the education of their disadvantaged preschool children.[31] During this period, parents of 85 disadvantaged children in 4 preschool classes met weekly with specially selected kindergarten teachers in their child's preschool classroom. At individual meetings with the teacher, each family was given materials and instruction for their use with the child in the home. The following week, these materials were exchanged for new ones and again the parents had a short conference with the teachers.

At the end of the 4-month pilot period, the children were tested and records of meetings were evaluated. It was concluded that, when guided and provided with meaningful material, most of the parents were happy and successful in helping their children. However, such help was not found to make significant changes in measures of the children's intelligence.

A new population of 68 kindergarten children was selected the following year with a plan for 3 consecutive years of experimental work with their parents. The parent participation program followed the pattern used in the pilot year, but meetings were held over 6 months, every second week. It was again confirmed that parents are ready to cooperate, even though they have to make the effort to come to get the materials. There were no significant differences between attendance of boys' and girls' parents, although a significantly greater number of boys' parents agreed initially to participate in the program.

Children in all classes had been involved in an early reading instruction program in the kindergarten. At the end of the year, 5 tests of reading achievement were given: reading of words, reading of stories, reading fluency, story content, and relationships in a story. On all 5 measures, children whose parents had been part of the experiment performed significantly better (p>.01) than their matched controls with whom no special parent contacts had been made. On intelligence tests, however, there were no significant differences between the experimental and control groups. Smilansky suggests 2 possible explanations: either reading training does not affect intelligence measures, or culturally disadvantaged parents are unable to affect the general intelligence level of their children through instruction.

Disadvantaged Parents (Lombard) A more concentrated effort to incorporate parents of disadvantaged preschool children in the educational process is the objective of a study by Lombard of the Hebrew University.[32] Working from the premise that children's educational deficits begin at home, this study sets forth a program of home instruction for preschoolers where mothers are the prime educators. Patterned after a similar project conducted by Tannenbaum of Teachers College, Columbia University, with first-graders,[33] the program involves a highly structured series of lessons which can be administered by the mother. Instructional materials are brought to the mother at home by an aide drawn from the same community and trained for her work by the project director.

The program includes a variety of exercises relating to formal language, sensory discrimination, and problem-solving skills. Five 20-minute daily lessons compose a week's work, and the aide visits once weekly to bring new materials and to receive reports on the previous week's activity.

The study is scheduled for 5 years. During the second year, 48 teachers of 4-year-olds incorporated the instructional materials into their classroom programs. Thus, the effectiveness of the materials could be examined under 2 totally different sets of conditions.

The primary research objectives of the study are

1 To examine the effects of a highly structured sequential program on

the intellectual and social development of educationally disadvantaged children.

2 To compare the effects of the program when taught by mothers in
the home as against its use by teachers in the classroom.

3 To investigate the optimum point of entry for such a program. It is
hypothesized that age 4 is best, but the program will also be started
with 5- and 6-year-old children.

4 To investigate the optimum length of instruction for each age group.
The full program consists of 3 years of instruction, but the effects of
either 2 years or one year of instruction will also be examined.

A second, but no less important, research objective involves the
examination of peripheral effects of the program, such as changes in
parental attitudes, the impact on the aides and their families, spillover
effects to siblings, and impact on the local community.

Although immediate measures of success will relate to the instructional materials used, the final results will refer to school success at
the end of second grade. Toward this end, yearly measures will be
made of the children's progress until the conclusion of second grade.

Statistical results of the first year's instruction are not yet available,
but records made by aides, teachers, and the field coordinator indicate
that the program is popular among the participating families (only 3
families dropped out). Teachers of the children instructed at home report that they distinguish themselves in ability and enthusiasm, especially when compared with their uninstructed counterparts.

Parent Education (Feitelson) A similar technique involving direct
work with mothers, but with somewhat different objectives, has been
under study by Feitelson,[34] who observed that young children from
Arab countries frequently do not play freely with toys or materials at
hand. Investigation of this observation showed that in many of the
cultures in which the children had been brought up, play was actually
frowned upon and in some cases forbidden.

In an attempt to promote creative activity in preschool children,
Feitelson developed a series of lessons, using simple, commonly found
household materials. The lessons were administered by University students in the children's homes, once a week. All the materials used
were left with the child for his own use following each lesson. Results
of this small study (N = 19) were very encouraging, and Feitelson is
working to expand the lesson series and to include the mother, rather
than a student, as the instructor. This is likely to be a formidable task,

since it is most frequently the mother herself who has actively inhibited play activity in her child.

Home Instruction Techniques (Ortar)   Gina Ortar, also of the Hebrew University of Jerusalem, has been experimenting with home instruction techniques for fostering intellectual development in children aged 14–17 months.[35] A sample of 90 infants (45 experimental and 45 controls) was selected from homes in which the mother has a maximum of 8 years of schooling. First-year student teachers in a nearby teacher-training institute visited the experimental homes 3 times a week for an hour of talk and play with the infants. The students were given regular guidance and instructions by the research staff throughout the 8-month period of the study.

It was hypothesized that there would be a significant difference in development between the experimental infants and their matched controls, who received no special attention. Results of this study are not yet available, but the students reported that they found the mothers enthusiastic and cooperative throughout.

Assessment of Behavior

Intellectual Deficiency Predictors (Szold Institute)   The problem of the precursors of intellectual deficiencies was the subject of a 5-year study conducted by Sarah Smilansky from the Henrietta Szold Institute in collaboration with Dr. Zvi Shamir of the Hadassah Medical School and Dr. Thanstein of the Ministry of Health.[36] Five hundred families, half of whom were of European origin, the other half whose origins were in Arab countries, were included in the sample. The study began in 1965 and followed the 500 infants from birth through kindergarten. The central objectives of the study were

1   To study the emotional, physical, social, and intellectual aspects of the processes of growth and development of Israeli children of various social classes and ethnic groups in different types of surroundings.
2   To investigate in the above groups the formation, extent, nature, and time of appearance of the intellectual lag.
3   To relate different aspects of the growth processes and child-rearing patterns to the social and cultural background.
4   To find the relationship of physical growth and development to intellectual growth and development.

Data collected include regular interviews with the mother from the time of pregnancy, medical and psychological examination, and observation of the children and their families. Most of the children have completed kindergarten, and final results of the study should be available in the near future.

Intellectual Functioning Predictors (Greenbaum)　A second study dealing with the precursors of intellectual functioning was conducted by Greenbaum of the Hebrew University, who made a comparative assessment of the reinforcing environment of infants.[37]

The purpose of the study was to assess the stimuli and reinforcements afforded the child in different child-rearing environments and to determine the child's response to the environment. The population consisted of male infants in 5 child-rearing environments: baby home (institutional), Bedouin Arab, kibbutz (collective), lower-class city, and middle-class city. Within each environment, children aged 2, 4, 7, and 11 months were observed.

The method used was a 24-hour observation of the child and all his interactions with his environment. An observation manual containing definitions of all behavior categories was used in the study. The results of this study should soon be available.

Standardized Test Adaptation (Hogen)　A major problem in assessing preschool children's progress has been the lack of appropriate locally standardized measurement instruments. In an attempt to find these, the Ministry of Education adapted the Caldwell Preschool Inventory for use in Hebrew with Israeli children.[38]

Primary objectives of the study were listed as follows:

1　To develop a test which would serve as a diagnostic instrument to identify areas of difficulty faced by individual children in the preschool years. Following such diagnosis, it was hypothesized that appropriate corrective measures could be taken by the classroom teacher.

2　To test the effectiveness of corrective teaching. Secondary objectives dealt with the effectiveness of prekindergarten education for kindergarten children, sex differences, and a comparison of test results with scores on the Draw-A-Man test.

In November 1968, 240 children aged 4 and 5, divided equally between advantaged and disadvantaged populations, were tested on a full translation of the Caldwell Preschool Inventory. All children were retested in June 1969 at the end of the school year, using a slightly revised and shortened version of the test. Five examiners administered the test to all the children both times and, in addition, Hogen administered the Draw-A-Man test to all children.

It was found that the Caldwell Preschool Inventory can be used diagnostically with 4- and 5-year-olds to yield both a general score and specific ratings for specific areas of functioning. Where corrective instruction was given following pretests, it was possible to measure the effects of such instruction. No differences were found between boys and girls, and previous preschool experience appeared to benefit only children of high socioeconomic background. A correlation was found between scores on the Caldwell Preschool Inventory and Draw-A-Man, but it was too low for confident use as a predictive measure.

The test was developed as an aid to teaching, and it was suggested that teachers be allowed to use it in the regular school setting. It was also suggested that further research be undertaken to examine the possibility of using the test as a predictor of first-grade achievement. At present, a limited number of qualified teachers are using the test with their pupils for diagnostic purposes.

CONCLUSION

The story of early childhood schooling in Israel is intimately linked with the history of the Israeli nation. From the beginning, education has been an integral part of the new nation's struggle for social survival and its search for cultural identity. Largely through education, Israel has attempted to absorb a threefold increase in its population—an increase characterized by extraordinary cultural diversity represented by more than 70 different languages—and to provide the means by which this varied population can share equally in the challenges and opportunities of a society rapidly moving toward increased industrialization.

This task is not yet complete. Though steadily declining in overall magnitude in recent years, the continuing waves of immigrants to Israel still include large numbers of Jews from Moslem countries, and the birth rate among Oriental Jews remains higher than the rest of the population. That the efforts to create national and cultural unity may claim a measure of success, however, is attested to by the fact that Israel has experienced no significant social or cultural unrest. And it must be remembered that Israel's efforts have spanned barely a quarter of a century, years marked by continual, and expensive, conflict with its surrounding neighbors. Present indications are that the problem of coping with sheer numbers might well be on the upswing once more. The steady stream of immigrants now coming from the USSR could expand to a flood, depending on future Russian policy toward emigration by its large population of Jews.

The evolution of government policy in education testifies to the new country's responsiveness to the continuing challenge. The revised policy of the Ministry of Education and Culture—its recognition of the complexity of the country's educational needs and its acknowledgment that the diversity of the population demands equal diversity in response—has already moved the educational system in new directions. Previously noted for its uniformity, and even rigidity, the educational system reflects a new variety and flexibility.

At the preschool level, the revised policy has stimulated the search for new programs and organizational structures which will be more effective in preparing the young child for the demands and opportunities of his later schooling. That progress to date has been limited is due in large part to the gap which always exists between policy and development work, and between new developments and ongoing practice. Many of the new proposals call for dramatic changes in the roles of institutions and of the people who compose them. The tradition of the separation of early childhood schooling from the mainstream, both organizationally and functionally, has resulted in considerable resistance to the proposals calling for a new K-2 institution and for more cognitively oriented programs. The Ministry is aware of the nature of this resistance and has initiated special training courses to prepare future and in-service teachers in the new approaches.

To date, the scope of educational research in Israel has been both limited and fragmentary, in part because of the restricted funds available for such activities. It has proceeded without an overarching and comprehensive framework which would clarify the interactions among cultural patterns, social organization, personality development, and learning processes. Several important areas have been largely ignored. For example, little or no research on the problem of language development and deficiencies in Israeli children has been undertaken. Similarly, scant attention has been paid to the emotional development of children—the relationship of self-concept and ego strength to the individual's success, both in school and in society.

As in the United States, the challenge of the future lies in the con-

tinued search for more effective means of enhancing the development
of children and of stimulating positive social change. As in the United
States, the early years are recognized as significant for educational
stimulation. However, Israel also is committed to a fully developed
educational system and to the production of leaders, especially in the
sciences. Consequently, the costs are enormous. It remains to be seen
whether resources commensurate with the challenging problem of
early schooling, and especially as these pertain to immigrant children,
will be allocated. It will be difficult to make the necessary commitment without some shift in priorities, a move that is exceedingly difficult for a country seeking to move forward rapidly and simultaneously
on so many fronts.

NOTES

1 Aharon F. Kleinberger, *Society, Schools and Progress in Israel*, Per-
gamon Press, London, 1969.

2 Morris B. Gross, "Israeli Disadvantaged," *Teachers College Record*,
vol. 72, 1970, pp. 105–110; and Hebrew University, "The Function
of Education and Social Integration in Israel, Summary of Experience
and Research Activities, January 1970," in *Education in Israel, Report of the Select Subcommittee on Education*, 91st US Congress,
2d session, August, 1970.

3 Ibid.

4 Kleinberger, op. cit.

5 Ibid.

6 Ibid., and Moshe and Sarah Smilansky, "Intellectual Advancement
of Culturally Disadvantaged Children: An Israeli Approach for Research and Action," *International Review of Education*, vol. 13, 1967,
pp. 410–428.

7 Hebrew University, op. cit.

8 Kleinberger, op. cit.

9 Ibid.

10 Ibid.

11 Population and public education figures are drawn from the Central
Bureau of Statistics, The Ministry of Education and Culture, *Jediot
bestatistika chinuchit* [Information on Educational Statistics 1969/70],
May 1970. Those having to do with preschool education refer only
to children and classes registered with the Ministry of Education
and do not include the unknown but large numbers of privately
run "unrecognized" preschools for 3- and 4-year-olds. In the summer of 1969, a new law was enacted whereby these privately run

schools will also come under the supervision of the Ministry. This will make detailed information available on the number and quality of private preschools and will insure a minimal standard of care and education.

12   Ministry of Education and Culture, *Letochnit ha-avoda began haye-ladim* [Work Programs for Kindergartens], Handbook 2, Ministry of Education and Culture, Jerusalem, 1966.

13   N. Naftali, *Hashita ha-intensivit: Hanchot vegishot* [The Intensive System: Underlying Assumptions and Approaches], Ministry of Education and Culture, Department of Supervision of Kindergartens, Tel Aviv, January 1968.

14   Kibbutz Ayelet Hashahar, "The Kibbutz," in *Education in Israel, Report of the Select Subcommittee on Education*, House Committee on Education and Labor, 91st US Congress, 2d session, August 1970; Joseph S. Bentwich, *Education in Israel*, Routledge & Kegan Paul, London, 1965; and Ivor Kraft, "A 'New Man' in the Kibbutz? A Review of Recent Writings on the Israel Collective Settlements," *Teachers College Record*, vol. 68, April 1967, pp. 558–595.

15   Bruno Bettelheim, *Children of the Dream*, Macmillan, London, 1969.

16   Bentwich, op. cit.

17   Peter B. Neubauer (ed.), *Children in Collectives, Child-Rearing Aims and Practices in the Kibbutz*, Charles C Thomas, Springfield, Ill., 1965, and Bentwich, op. cit.

18   Randolph L. Braham, *Israel—A Modern Education System*, US Government Printing Office, Washington, 1966.

19   Stephen Wilson, "Educational Changes in the Kibbutz," *Comparative Education*, vol. 5, 1969, pp. 67–72.

20   Kleinberger, op. cit.

21   Wilson, op. cit.; Bentwich, op. cit.; and Los Angeles Times, Dec. 7, 1971, part 1-A, p. 4.

22   Sarah Smilansky, L. Shefatya, and N. Doran, "Nisui longitudinali behora-at kriya leyeladei gan hova" [A Longitudinal Experiment in the Teaching of Reading to Kindergarten Children], Henrietta Szold Institute, National Institute for Research in the Behavioral Sciences, Jerusalem, May 1970.

23   D. Lipschitz, *Nisui kriya began hayeladim* [A Reading Experiment in the Kindergarten] Ministry of Education, Curriculum Guidance Office for Elementary Education and Teacher Training, Tel Aviv, 1965.

24   Sarah Smilansky, *The Effect of Sociodramatic Play on Disadvantaged Preschool Children*, Wiley, New York, 1968.

25   Sarah Smilansky, "The Effect of Certain Learning Conditions on the Progress of Disadvantaged Children of Kindergarten Age," *Journal of School Psychology*, vol. 4, 1966, pp. 68–81.

26 R. Bilsky-Cohen and N. Melnick, "Pituah intellectuali shel yeladim teunei tipuah be-emtzaut tnua yotzeret" [Intellectual Development of Disadvantaged Children by Means of Creative Movement], Midyear Report, Hebrew University of Jerusalem, Jerusalem, February 1970.

27 Ruth Ben-Shaul, producer, Instructional Television Centre of the Ministry of Education and Culture, personal communication, 1971.

28 D. Feitelson and S. Krown, "The Effects of Heterogeneous Grouping and Compensatory Measures on Culturally Disadvantaged Pre-School Children in Israel," Progress Report, Hebrew University of Jerusalem, Jerusalem, 1969.

29 J. Aschel, K. Benjamini, C. Greenbaum, and Z. Klein, "The Study of the Effect of Integration on Interaction among Preschool Children," Draft and Proposal, Hebrew University of Jerusalem, Jerusalem, 1970.

30 Sarah Smilansky, "A Program to Demonstrate Ways of Using a Year of Kindergarten to Promote Cognitive Abilities, Impart Basic Information, and Modify Attitudes Which Are Essential for Scholastic Success of Culturally Deprived Children in Their First Two Years of School," Progress Report, Henrietta Szold Institute, National Institute for Research in the Behavioral Sciences, Jerusalem, 1964.

31 Sarah Smilansky, "The Relative Importance of Different Frameworks (Family and Kindergarten) in Promoting Cognitive Abilities In Young Children from Culturally Deprived Strata," Progress Reports 1966–1968, Henrietta Szold Institute, National Institute for Research in the Behavioral Sciences, Jerusalem, 1966–1968.

32 Avima Lombard, "Home Instruction Program for Preschool Youngsters," Interim Report, Hebrew University of Jerusalem, Jerusalem, March 1971.

33 A. J. Tannenbaum, "An Evaluation of STAR: A Non-Professional Tutoring Program," *Teachers College Record*, vol. 69, 1968, pp. 433–448.

34 D. Feitelson and A. Herzberg, "Individual Tutoring as a Way of Developing the Ability to Play among Middle Eastern Preschool Children in Israel," paper presented at 6th Conference of the International Council for Children's Play, Turin, Italy, May 1968.

35 Gina Ortar, "Ziruz hitpatchut hasichlit shel peutot be-emtzaut tipul kavua hanitan al yadei naarot lomdot" [Acceleration of Intellectual Development of Infants by Means of Regularly Scheduled Activity with Female Students], Midyear Report, Hebrew University of Jerusalem, Jerusalem, February 1970.

36 Henrietta Szold Institute, "National Institute for Research in the Behavioral Sciences, Report on Activities, 1964–1966," Henrietta Szold Institute, Jerusalem, June 1967.

37 C. W. Greenbaum, "Assessment of the Reinforcing Environment in

Preschool Children," Progress Report, Hebrew University of Jerusalem, Jerusalem, December 1968. (US Department of Health, Education and Welfare, Office of Education Grant No. 6-1-7071308-4465.)

38   M. Hogen, *Mivhan hesegim legil harach* [Achievement Test for Preschool Children], Final Report, Ministry of Education, Tel Aviv, 1970.

APPENDIX A

|I|D|E|A| Nursery School Survey

Developed for the Research Division of the Institute for Development of Educational Activities, Inc. by Norma Feshbach, M. Frances Klein, Jerrold M. Novotney and Judith Ramirez with the assistance of Alice Burnett, David Elkind, Else Hjertholm, Bernice McLaren, Edna Mitchell, Frances Prindle, Lois Sauer, Joanna Williams, Robert Williams, and Edgar A. Quimby.

Director, Administrator, Teacher Interview
(Circle which person is interviewed)
One per school

1. *Descriptive data* (order of items may be varied to fit the situation)
   a. School _____
   b. City and state _____
   c. Age range of school _____
   d. Number of children in school _____
   e. Number of classes/groups _____
   f. Control of school:
      College or university laboratory _____
      Independent _____
      Parent cooperative _____
      Parochial or church controlled _____
      Public [Specify controlling agency(s)]
         Local _____
         State _____
         Federal _____
      Other _____
   g. Program emphases: (Check as many as apply. Star main emphasis.)
      Behavior modification _____
      Compensatory education _____
      Custodial or day care _____
      Exceptional children's center _____
      Montessori _____
      Parent education _____
      Preparation of paraprofessionals _____
      Program development & research _____
      Teacher training _____
      Other _____
   h. Size of town where school is located: (Locate and mark location of
      school on map)
      Metropolitan (100,000 or more)
         (1) Central city (city limits) _____
         (2) Old suburb _____
         (3) New suburb _____
      Large—Medium city (over 25,000) _____ Small town _____
   i. Range of socioeconomic status of parents _____
   j. Primary source(s) of funds _____
   k. Amount of tuition charged _____
   l. How much of a waiting period before child may enter _____
   m. How often director on site _____

2. How important, in your opinion, are the following areas to your program?

	Low	Medium	High
Academic skills (reading, writing, drawing, arithmetic)			
Arts and creative expression			
Cognitive-intellectual development			
Concept acquisition (training in concepts of time, color, size)			
Emotional development (confidence, self-esteem)			
Language skills: oral development			
reading and vocabulary development			
Motor skills (large muscle)			
Sensory awareness			
Sensory motor skills (visual, auditory, muscle training)			
Social-interpersonal skills (cooperation, rules)			
Verbalizing feelings			
(Other—specify)			

3. What do you consider to be the primary function(s) of your school? (Child care, readiness for school, child-development program, etc.)

4. What are the specific objectives of your program?

5. Is your program evaluated? If so, how?

6. What forms of evaluation of student growth are used by the school and/or teachers? (Teacher observation, standardized tests, sociometric data, etc.)

7. Is any reporting done by the school and/or teacher to parents? (Conferences, written reports, phone calls, informal talks, etc.) If so, how often?

8. TEACHING PERSONNEL FOR ENTIRE SCHOOL (*Note:* Be as specific as you can regarding the numbers appropriate for each entry.)	Number	High school graduate	Some college	College degree	Graduate degree	Formal training in early child-hood education	Years experience in nursery education	Other teaching experience
Director, Head Teacher								
Teachers								
Assistant Teachers								
Aides								
A. Aides not related to children								
B. Parent aides								
Specialists (specify)								
Consultants (specify)								
(For remainder, record only pertinent information)								
Nutritionist								
Housekeeper								
Custodian								
Others								

9. Are your facilities and materials shared by other groups? If so, what other groups use them and how often?

10. The following items are possible curricular areas and activities which might be found in programs for young children. We would like to have an indication of how frequently they occur in your program.

Curricular Area and Activity	Frequency			
	Daily	Frequently	Occasionally	Rarely or Never
Curricular Areas:				
Arithmetic				
Informal				
Formal				
Art				
Foreign Languages (specify)				
Language				
Informal				
Formal				
Music				
Informal				
Formal				
Musical Instrument Instruction				
Reading Readiness				
Informal				
Formal				
Reading				
Science				
Informal				
Formal				
Social Studies				
Informal				
Formal				

(continued)

10. (Continued)

Curricular Area and Activity	Frequency			
	Daily	Frequently	Occasionally	Rarely or Never
Other (specify)				

Activities:
Blocks				
Carpentry (wood work)				
Cooking				
Dramatization and Role-Playing				
Group Games (organized)				
Informal Rest				
Naps				
Nature Walks				
Outdoor Play				
Rhythms				
Story Time				
Trips				
Other (specify)				

11   To what extent do parents participate in the daily activities? (Required, enage, discouraged, etc.) How do they participate? (Assistant teachers, resources, no involvement with children, etc.)

12. Do you organize any parent meetings? If so, what types (PTA, work parties, discussion groups)? How often are they held? What is your average attendance?

Type	How often held	Average Attendance

13. Do you attempt to obtain any information about the child and/or his family when he registers? If so, how (written forms, administrator interview, teacher conference, etc.)?

14. Are there entrance requirements or criteria students or parents must meet —(medical, racial, intellectual, etc.)? If so, what are they?

15. What are the approximate percentages of children enrolled in your school on varying days?
    _____ All day every day   _____ other (specify)
    _____ Half day every day   _____
    _____ Monday, Wednesday, & Friday half day   _____
    _____ Tuesday and Thursday half day   _____
    _____

16. What is the average adult per child ratio for the school? _____

17. Describe facility of school
    a. Indoor (size of room, appearance, restroom facilities, sinks)
    b. Outdoor (appearance, apparatus, materials, size, safety)
    c. Overall physical facilities

18. What are the major problems or issues which your school and/or teachers face?

19. What would you consider to be unique about and/or particularly successful in your school?

Nursery School Survey
Classroom Observation Form

(One per teacher observed)

I. Descriptive Data

Date _____

1. School _____

2. City and state _____

3. Teacher _____

4. Age range of this group _____

5. Time period this group in session _____

6. Number of children in group: Girls ⎯⎯⎯⎯⎯ Boys ⎯⎯⎯⎯⎯

7. Adult/child ratio for classroom ⎯⎯⎯⎯⎯⎯⎯⎯⎯⎯⎯⎯

8. Number of aides and other personnel ⎯⎯⎯⎯⎯⎯⎯⎯⎯⎯

9. Teacher professional preparation and background ⎯⎯⎯⎯⎯

⎯⎯⎯⎯⎯⎯⎯⎯⎯⎯⎯⎯⎯⎯⎯⎯⎯⎯⎯⎯

Observer name ⎯⎯⎯⎯⎯⎯⎯⎯⎯⎯⎯⎯⎯⎯⎯⎯⎯

II. Observation Time
   A. Length of observation
   B. Time of day observed

III. Collect daily schedule of teacher—note variability in program

IV. Curricular Activities
    (Please rate all activities observed)

| Curricular Area and Activity | Structure | | | |
	Highly regulated	Some structure	Unstructured	Not observed
Curricular Areas:				
Arithmetic				
Informal				
Formal				
Art				
Foreign Languages (specify)				
Language				
Informal				
Formal				
Music				
Informal				
Formal				
Musical Instrument Instruction				

(continued)

IV. Curricular Activities (Continued)

Curricular Area and Activity	Structure			
	Highly regulated	Some structure	Unstructured	Not observed
Reading Readiness Informal				
Formal				
Reading				
Science Informal				
Formal				
Social Studies Informal				
Formal				
Other (specify)				
Activities: Blocks				
Carpentry (wood work)				
Cooking				
Dramatization and Role-Playing				
Group Games (organized)				
Informal Rest				
Naps				
Nature Walks				
Outdoor Play				
Rhythms				
Story Time				
Trips				
Other (specify)				

V. Materials and Equipment

	(Check everything which is in sight)	
	Present Indoor	Present Outdoor
Furniture and Facilities: Bulletin boards		
Chairs: A. adult		
B. adult rocker		
C. child-size straight chairs		
D. child-size rockers		
Chalk board		
Cots		
Cubby or locker for personal items		
Desks for working		
Mats for resting		
Phonograph		
Piano		
Running water		
Tables for working		
Television		
Toilets		
Materials: Animals (real) (specify)		

(continued)

V. Materials and Equipment (Continued)

	(Check everything which is in sight)	
	Present Indoor	Present Outdoor
Balls		
Blocks (unit, table)		
Blocks, crates (floor)		
Books: a. texts (preprimers, primers)		
b. library (picture)		
Carriages and buggies		
Clay, play dough, plasticene		
Climbing apparatus (jungle gym, bars)		
Collage materials		
Cooking materials: a. toys		
b. real (adult)		
Crayons		
Dolls and accessories		
Dress up clothes & accessories		
Easels (& all materials used with easels) paints		
Filmstrips		
Finger paints		
Housekeeping toys (materials for dramatic play, e.g., dishes)		
Jump ropes		
Math materials (abacus, clocks, ruler, number games)		
Mats for working		
Mechanical toys (take-apart toys)		
Movies		
Music listening (records, tapes, etc.)		

(continued)

V. Materials and Equipment (Continued)

	(Check everything which is in sight)	
	Present Indoor	Present Outdoor
Programmed materials (learning games) language, math, reading		
Puppets		
Puzzles: A. wood inlay		
B. cardboard		
Riding equipment: A. bicycles		
B. tricycles		
C. scooters		
D. wagons		
E. cars		
F. other (specify)		
Rhythm instruments (e.g., bells, castanets, cymbals, drums, maracas, rhythm sticks)		
Sand (all toys & accessories)		
Science materials and corner (e.g., battery, flower boxes, prism, seeds, globe, magnifier)		
Slides		
Store equipment		
Stuffed animals		
Swings		
Table toys (blocks, games, bingo, lego)		
Tools (hoes, rakes, shovels)		
Transparencies		
Trucks, cars, trains, boats (small—not rideable) A. Highly defined toys		
B. Creative play equipment		
Water play area		
Water toys		

(continued)

V. Materials and Equipment (Continued)

	(Check everything which is in sight)	
	Present Indoor	Present Outdoor
Wood working materials (bench, clamp, hammer, etc.)		
Workbooks (nonprogrammed materials)		

VI. Overall Ratings
   Facilities and Equipment

	Please check both columns for questions 1 and 2	
1. Variety of equipment and materials	Indoor	Outdoor
Minimum equipment & materials: sparse		
Some equipment & materials, somewhat below average		
Moderate amount of equipment & materials, adequate		
Ample materials, wide breadth of materials		
Very well equipped, rich array of materials		
2. Quantity of equipment and materials		
Very limited, insufficient for number of children		
Adequate amount, turns for children required, but not unduly frustrating		
Ample amount for number of children in the group		

3. Space within school and classrooms
  _____ Cramped, crowded, much too little
  _____ Insufficient for program and number of children
  _____ Adequate, but not spacious
  _____ Large, open, spacious
4. Ventilation of classrooms
  _____ Inadequate, close, stuffy
  _____ Adequate, comfortable classrooms
  _____ Drafty, too open and airy

5. Physical surroundings in classroom (location, decoration, color, etc.)
  _____ Dingy and depressing
  _____ Neither dingy nor cheerful
  _____ Cheerful and sunny

6. Organization of room
  _____ No obvious organization, chaotic
  _____ Rigid organization, little flexibility
  _____ Organized, but inefficient/ineffective (interferes with movement)
  _____ Allows for freedom of movement with little disruption to others

7. Condition of equipment in classroom
  _____ Poor; in need of repairs and paint, dirty
  _____ Adequate, usable, patched
  _____ Good, has been repaired, kept up
  _____ Excellent, new equipment

8. Safety of classroom
  _____ Very unsafe, disrepair, fire hazards
  _____ Meets minimum safety standards
  _____ Adequate safety precautions
  _____ High safety standards in operation

9. Access to outdoors
  _____ Rarely (because of weather, space, etc.)
  _____ Daily walks—but outdoors not readily available
  _____ At specified times during week/month
  _____ Daily, but scheduled and routine
  _____ Daily, whenever desired

10. Outdoor area
  _____ None attached to school
  _____ Some space attached to school, somewhat crowded
  _____ Large, open, accessible

Classroom Activities
1. Noise level
   _____ Of a chaotic nature, noisy to the point of discomfort
   _____ Reasonable amount of noise
   _____ Unnaturally quiet for preschool

2. Routines and rules
   _____ High emphasis on routines (proper toileting, manners, frequent verbalization by teacher on procedures and rules)
   _____ Some emphasis on routines but fairly casual attitudes
   _____ Little or no emphasis on routines, rules rarely mentioned; very casual

3. Emphasis on academic preparation and academic skills
   _____ Academic skills main goal and activity of the program
   _____ Materials and curricula type projects are an important part of the program (i.e., most Headstart programs)
   _____ Some emphasis on academic preparation, other goals important
   _____ Academic materials and activities quite secondary
   _____ Academic, educational activities are absent, or discouraged

4. Degree of integration and organization
   _____ Disorganized, program seems unplanned
   _____ Moderate organization and planning
   _____ Coherent, directed, smooth transitions and implementation of program

5. Variety of activities available to children in the program
   _____ Few activities
   _____ Moderate number of activities
   _____ Many activities

6. Children's use of space
   _____ Hampered, restricted
   _____ Use most areas appropriately
   _____ Use every amount available

7. Individualization of program
   _____ No evidence of individualization; entirely group-oriented
   _____ Individuals recognized, but used to forward group activity primarily; no diagnosis and prescription of individual needs occurring
   _____ Limited individualization; little diagnosis and prescription for individual needs
   _____ Much individualization evident; diagnosis and prescription for children's needs evident

Interaction

1. Degree of teacher-child interaction
   _____ Very little interaction although physical proximity may be high (i.e., teacher passes out food but does not interact with children)
   _____ Some degree of physical or verbal interaction (pats on head, body, some individual verbal recognition of children)
   _____ A high degree of either physical or verbal interaction present (i.e., holds child on lap; talks intimately with child)
   _____ Little interaction, but teacher readily available and active when needed

2. Quality of teacher-child interaction
   _____ Cold, critical, disinterested, punitive
   _____ Moderately warm and interested in children
   _____ Very warm, supportive and accepting

3. Degree of child-child interaction
   _____ Low—most children rarely interact with each other (parallel rather than interactive play)
   _____ Moderate amount of child-child interaction, considerable parallel play
   _____ High—most children actively engaged with other children

4. Quality of child-child interaction
   _____ Aggressive, negative interaction
   _____ Largely aggressive, negative interaction
   _____ Passive, docile interaction
   _____ Largely shared, cooperative, positive interaction
   _____ Shared, cooperative, positive interaction

5. Degree of child-teacher interaction
   _____ Low, children rarely or never initiate contact with teacher
   _____ Moderate amount
   _____ High, many children initiate contact with teacher

6. Quality of child-teacher interaction
   _____ Children hesitate to initiate contacts
   _____ Children contact largely out of frustration
   _____ Children freely contact teacher as needed, primarily for routine requests and permission
   _____ Children freely contact teacher as needed, primarily for resource and enrichment

7. Interpersonal aggression
   _____ Aggression strongly inhibited

_____ Moderately disapproved of
_____ Reasoned and discussed
_____ Ignored
_____ Permitted

8. Interest, activity, and engagement of children
_____ Very little activity, lethargy
_____ Children generally busy, not greatly involved
_____ Children busily engaged, involved in task

9. Interest, activity & engagement of teachers	Little involvement with children or program	Busy with routines, etc., but little engagement with children	Moderately engaged with children & program	Highly engaged with children & program	Unobtrusive with children but engaged in observation & program
10. Interest, activity & engagement of aides					

	Subdued, detached emotionally	Moderately happy, enthusiastic	Very enthusiastic, cheerful, eager
11. Mood & morale of children			
12. Mood & morale of teacher			
13. Mood & morale of teacher aides			

Teacher Behavior
1. Locus of control and decision making

_____ Group and class teacher controlled
_____ Children have opportunities to make decisions but teacher directs most of the time
_____ Children have many opportunities to make decisions

2. Role of teacher
_____ Authority in charge, highly directive
_____ Directive, but unobtrusively
_____ Resource for children to use
_____ Little direction or interaction with children unless necessary

3. Type of reinforcement used most frequently by teacher (May check more than 1)

_____ Group pressure

_____ Loss of privilege

_____ Scolding, warning, threatening

_____ Punitive isolation within or outside of classroom

_____ Physical punishment

_____ Teacher ignored situation

_____ Verbal praise

_____ Physical rewards (smile, pats, nods of head)

_____ Tangible rewards (candy, toy)

_____ Diverting child to new activity

_____ Talking to the child (reasoning)

_____ Planned time-out (temporary withdrawal)

_____ No occasion for discipline occurred or no basis for judgment

_____

_____

_____

_____

_____

_____

_____

VII. Describe grouping of children observed. Note size (large, small, individual), frequency (fluid, fixed), formation (teacher-directed, self-selection), and structure (age, sex, etc.) of groups.

VIII. Describe the cross-cultural ethnic composition of the group.

IX. Describe or collect any materials which look promising. Note why you consider them to be promising.

X. Uniqueness of program. Note anything of unusual interest (Problem areas or success areas).

XI. Observations (Additional observations and impressions may be recorded on reverse side of printed pages.)

APPENDIX B

Recommendations of the Plowden Report Regarding Nursery Education*

(i) There should be a large expansion of nursery education, and a start should be made as soon as possible.

(ii) Nursery education should be available to children at any time after the beginning of the school year after which they reach the age of three until they reach the age of compulsory schooling.

(iii) Nursery education should be available either for a *morning* or *afternoon* session for five days a week except that over the country as a whole provision should be made for 15 percent of children to attend both a morning and afternoon session.

(iv) The take up of nursery places by children in special need should be carefully watched by local education authorities and by the Department of Education and Science so that further methods of persuasion can be used to bring in all children who are in need of nursery education.

(v) Low priority should be given to full-time nursery education for children whose mothers cannot satisfy the authorities that they have exceptionally good reasons for working.

(vi) Children should be introduced gradually to nursery education.

(vii) Nursery education should be provided in nursery groups of up to 20 places. More than one and up to three groups might be formed as one unit to be called a nursery centre or to be combined with day nurseries or clinics in children's centres.

(viii) The education of children over three in day nurseries should be the responsibility of the education rather than health departments.

* From: *Children and Their Primary Schools,* Report of the Central Advisory Council of Education, Her Majesty's Stationery Office, London, 1967, vol. I, pp. 132–33, para. 343.

121

(ix) All nursery groups should be under the ultimate supervision of a qualified teacher in the ratio of one qualified teacher to 60 places. The main day to day work of the groups should be undertaken by two year trained nursery assistants in the ratio of a minimum of one to every ten children. There should be at least one experienced nursery assistant in each group and where no teacher is always on the premises, one assistant able to cope with accidents and safety risks. Experienced assistants should be able to qualify on merit for a responsibility allowance.

(x) Nursery groups which are under the supervision of a teacher or head teacher of an adjoining primary school should be part of that school. Groups not attached to a school should form a single nursery centre with the other groups which are supervised by the same qualified teacher.

(xi) Until enough maintained places are available, local education authorities should be given power and be encouraged to give financial or other assistance to nursery groups run by non-profit making associations which in their opinion fill a need which they cannot meet. Voluntary groups, with or without help from public funds, should be subject to inspection by local education authorities and H.M. Inspectorate similar to that of the maintained nurseries.

(xii) Ideally, all services, including nursery, for the care of young children should be grouped together and placed near the children's homes and the primary schools. The planning of new areas and the rebuilding of old should take account of nursery education.

(xiii) Local authorities should undertake local surveys at an appropriate time to assess the net cost of extra accommodation needed to establish nursery provision in their area and to see how many qualified teachers will be available following changes in the age of entry to the first school.

INDEX